Jude's

ICE CREAM
& DESSERTS

Jude's

ICE CREAM
& DESSERTS

SCOOPS · BAKES SHAKES · SAUCES

BY **CHOW** AND **ALEX MEZGER**
WITH **GEORGINA FUGGLE**

PHOTOGRAPHY BY YUKI SUGIURA

KYLE BOOKS

This book is dedicated to the Jude's team, who have given so much of themselves to build an ice cream company that we can all be proud of.

An Hachette UK Company
www.hachette.co.uk

First published in Great Britain in 2019 by
Kyle Books, an imprint of Kyle Cathie Ltd
Carmelite House
50 Victoria Embankment
London EC4Y 0DZ
www.kylebooks.co.uk

Distributed in the US by Hachette Book Group, 1290 Avenue of the Americas, 4th and 5th Floors, New York, NY 10104.

Distributed in Canada by Canadian Manda Group, 664 Annette St., Toronto, Ontario, Canada M6S 2C8.

ISBN: 978 085783 534 5

10 9 8 7 6 5 4 3 2 1

Photographer: Yuki Sugiura
Recipes & Food Stylist: Georgina Fuggle
Props Stylist: Linda Berlin
Book Design: Studio Noel
Project Editor: Sophie Allen
Editorial assistant: Sarah Kyle
Project Producer: Laura Pink
Copywriter of introductions: Mary Horgan
Production: Gemma John and Nic Jones

A Cataloguing in Publication record for this title is available from the British Library.

Printed and bound in China

We would like to thank Cuisinart for the use of their ice-cream makers to develop and test recipes for this book.

CONTENTS

OUR STORY

Our dad was starting an ice cream company.

What began as a barely whispered idea had soon become a regular topic of conversation amongst the family, and in the space of a few months it was actually happening. Though it came completely out of the blue, we could make sense of it. He had often talked of making something with his own two hands, selling a real product to real people, and he's always loved great food. His mission was to make the greatest tasting ice cream in Britain.

He started small and set to work in our old dairy barn at home in Hampshire. Our mum soon joined him in the work and he decided to name the company after her. On 19 December 2002, he walked across the field to the village pub to sell his very first tubs of Jude's ice cream.

Soon the whole family joined in, mixing, churning and learning the craft of making really great ice cream using proper ingredients. Right from the beginning, we all approached our responsibilities with a blend of carefree enthusiasm and earnest rigour. With our growing team of brilliant individuals, we dedicated huge amounts of time and focus to studying and mastering our craft, refining our recipes, tasting and testing. We built relationships with suppliers of the best ingredients and equipment, intent on gaining an understanding of every intricate step of the process. We wanted to master it all, from the art of perfectly balancing flavours to the science of formulating recipes that achieve the optimum freezing point and smoothest texture.

From the start, we've been putting flavour first. Flavour is a delicate matter and there are very few overnight successes. Getting it right demands a commitment to exciting experimentation as well as continuous trial and error. We search high and low to gather quality ingredients with superb provenance, from West Country clotted cream and English sea salt to Madagascan vanilla and Colombian cacao. Our creamy milk comes from Matterley Farm, just down the road from our dairy in Hampshire, which is home to a herd of 220 Holstein Friesian grass-grazed cows.

Drawing inspiration from our rich British heritage and the exciting local food scene, as well as trips abroad, we're proud of the incredibly delicious scoops that we've dreamed up – from our classic Salted Caramel, to our oh-so-British Sipsmith Gin and Tonic, and our surprising limited edition Black Coconut. Over the years we've wanted to develop inclusive products, making dairy-free options that are suitable for vegans, such as our sorbets and dairy-free ice creams made using nut milk. It's a real thrill for us that our ice creams have been so well recognized. Early on, many of the best chefs in the country came knocking,

keen to put our scoops on their menus, and before long our tubs were on the shelves in some of the UK's best-loved supermarkets. To date, we've won 45 Great Taste awards, of which we couldn't be more proud.

We continue to reflect on why we do what we do. At its very heart, Jude's is all about bringing joy and delight to people through both making great ice cream and how we act as a company. It has always felt vital to look outward and give back, which is why we work with schools in our local community and with amazing organizations that do work that we couldn't do. We love supporting brilliant charities, including Spear, Naomi House and Home for Good, all of which champion children and young people in their own unique, impactful ways. And we really love the idea that when you're tucking into our ice cream, you're also putting smiles on faces and making a difference.

So, why a Jude's cookbook? We want to help you bring family and friends together around exciting and inspiring food. Great grub was always at the heart of our family growing up, with plenty of big celebrations that called for one and all to muck in and prepare a feast to get everyone fed. We vividly remember glorious vats of stew simmering away in giant Le Creuset dishes, and how our mum, Jude, proudly hung her hard-earned Cordon Bleu cookery course certificate on the kitchen wall to remind us (should we be in any doubt!) of her top-notch cooking credentials. We all delighted in the sweet stuff, too. As

children we grew up on brownies, banana ice cream, arctic rolls, trifles, fruit cake, gooseberry fool and – last but not least – granny's legendary and perfectly formed meringues.

We hope the recipes in these pages will inspire you to gather people together to catch up, celebrate, or simply be, all while indulging in delicious and inspiring homemade food. We wanted to share what we've learned over the years, so you can create some magic for your loved ones. Time and again, chefs, friends and fans ask us for tricks and tips on how to make seriously tasty ice cream, and now we're sharing our secrets. It's also about looking forward, bringing together new flavour combinations, recipe formulations and baking techniques.

It's been a real pleasure to weave this all together and to see it brought to life in one place. We couldn't be happier to have teamed up with Georgina Fuggle to do it. She's a great friend of the family and we've been collaborating with her for years. She's truly gifted at making homemade ice cream and perfect pudding pairings.

We'd love this to be your go-to book when your thoughts turn to everyone's favourite course – dessert – whether you're pairing a seasonal ice cream with fruit from the garden, whipping up a quick and healthy treat for little people or masterminding a showstopper for family and friends. We're so excited to share this with you.

Alex & Chow

A FEW

GENERAL TIPS

FREEZING ICE CREAM WITHOUT A MACHINE

Pour the mixture into a shallow, wide, freezer proof container and freeze for 1 hour, until the mixture freezes, forming a border around the edge. Break up the ice crystals with a fork or whisk and return to the freezer. Repeat this whisking every 30 minutes or so, until evenly set and too thick to fork. It should take 2–3 hours.

ICE-CREAM MACHINES

There are a few different varieties of ice-cream maker – some have an in-built freezer and others need you to freeze the bowl for 24 hours in advance. They also take different times to churn your ice cream, so please check the instructions for timings.

INGREDIENTS

The quality of ingredients used in these recipes make a big difference to the resulting flavour. We recommend that you find the best ingredients you can, in season where possible. Some recipes call for a vanilla pod – this is an expensive ingredient so be sure to get as much use from it as possible. Once you've removed the seeds, leave the pod in a warm spot to dry and then nestle it into a bag of sugar – it will flavour your sugar beautifully.

Here are some icons used throughout the book.

 Tips   Top tips   Vegan    No-Churn

CHAPTER 1

SCOOPS
DAIRY & VEGAN

We create and taste hundreds of recipes every year, and count
ourselves extremely lucky to have such a great job. The traditional
ice cream method starts with a crème anglaise made up from
milk, cream, eggs and sugar. These ingredients make up a creamy
custard base which is used in our Ultimate Vanilla recipe (page 14).
We could have written a whole book of ice cream flavours based
on this method, so if there is one recipe to master, this is the one.
We've also developed alternative methods that are interesting in
execution and delicious in taste. Our Salted Caramel (page 23)
starts off with a bubbling pot of rich caramel and builds from
there, our Matcha ice cream (page 31) requires no cooking
and our no-churn recipes use a higher cream and sugar
content to make them scoopable without churning.
Look out for our vegan collection featuring our
intense Double Dark Chocolate Ice Cream
(page 48) and the refreshingly summery
Watermelon and Strawberry
Granita (page 60).

THE ULTIMATE VANILLA ICE CREAM

This is the first flavour our dad churned, sampled and perfected in the old dairy barn at home. It's still his favourite and it's our best-selling scoop. An out-and-out classic, vanilla is the foundation of many an ice cream recipe, so it's more than worth getting it right. Once you have mastered this, you'll have a friend for life that you can adapt for a whole world of flavour experimentation.

SERVES 6
MAKES 1 LITRE (1¾ PINTS)

300ml (½ pint) double cream

300ml (½ pint) whole milk

1 vanilla pod, slit in half lengthways

A pinch of salt

6 medium egg yolks

100g (3½oz) golden caster sugar

TOP TIP

CLASSIC AFFOGATO
A strong, hot shot of espresso is poured over one or two scoops of vanilla ice cream and served immediately as the ice cream melts.

OLIVE OIL AND SALT
A scoop of vanilla ice cream served with nothing but a glug of extra virgin olive oil and a sprinkling of sea salt is a glorious and unexpected flavour match.

Pour the cream and milk into a small saucepan. Use the tip of a sharp knife to scrape the seeds from the vanilla pod and into the cream, along with the empty pod. Place the saucepan over a very gentle heat for 8–10 minutes and, when the cream is almost boiling, remove the pan from the heat and leave to cool for 20 minutes, allowing the vanilla to flavour the milk.

Meanwhile, using a wooden spoon, beat the salt, egg yolks and sugar together in a large mixing bowl for 2–3 minutes until light and uniform.

Remove the pod from the warm cream mixture and, working slowly, pour the mixture into the sugared yolks and continue to beat together until all is combined. Return the lot to a clean saucepan and cook over a gentle heat, stirring continuously, for up to 10 minutes. The mixture will eventually thicken to a custard consistency, just thick enough to coat the back of the wooden spoon. At this point, remove from the heat and transfer to a clean bowl (this prevents any further cooking). Set aside to cool for an hour.

Pour into an ice-cream machine and churn to a soft set following the manufacturer's instructions, or until the blade stops. Spoon the soft ice cream into an airtight, freezerproof container. Cover and put in the freezer for at least 4 hours, or preferably overnight, until firm.

Remove from the freezer and allow the ice cream to soften for 5–10 minutes before scooping.

HONEY, FIG AND THYME ICE CREAM

This little number sings in your mouth, thanks to the fresh, juicy figs. We've discovered they sit beautifully with honey and young thyme. The balance is just sweet enough, with a modern botanical twist thanks to the rich, earthy herb. First, make a delicious compôte from this trio, then blend it into the ice-cream base.

SERVES 8
MAKES 1.2 LITRES (2 PINTS)

300g (10½oz) ripe black figs, stalks removed and roughly chopped into 1–2cm (½–¾in) chunks

25g (1oz) soft dark brown sugar

2 tablespoons clear honey

3–4 thyme sprigs

Juice of ½ lemon

VANILLA BASE

350ml (12fl oz) double cream

250ml (9fl oz) whole milk

1 vanilla pod, slit in half lengthways

A pinch of salt

6 medium egg yolks

100g (3½oz) golden caster sugar

Pour the cream and milk into a small saucepan. Scrape the seeds from the vanilla pod into the cream, along with the empty pod. Place the saucepan over a very gentle heat for 8–10 minutes and, when the cream is almost boiling, remove from the heat and leave to cool for 20 minutes, allowing the vanilla to flavour the milk.

Meanwhile, make the fig purée. Gently heat the figs, sugar, honey and thyme sprigs in a small saucepan, stirring and squashing with a wooden spoon until the fruit starts to break down, about 5 minutes. Cover, reduce the heat and simmer for 10 minutes, stirring occasionally, until the figs break down and the mixture is thick and jam-like. Remove from the heat, pick out the thyme sprigs and stir through the lemon juice. Use a stick blender to purée the jam uniformly. Set aside to cool to room temperature.

Return to the vanilla base. Using a wooden spoon, beat the salt, egg yolks and sugar together in a large mixing bowl for 2–3 minutes until light and uniform. Remove the pod from the warm cream mixture and slowly pour it into the sugared yolks and continue to beat together until combined. Return the lot to a clean saucepan and cook over a gentle heat, stirring continuously, for up to 10 minutes. The mixture will thicken to a custard consistency, just thick enough to coat the back of the wooden spoon. At this point, remove from the heat and transfer to a clean bowl (this prevents any further cooking). Set aside to cool for 1 hour before stirring three-quarters of the fig purée through the ice-cream base.

Pour into an ice-cream machine and churn to a soft set following the manufacturer's instructions, or until the blade stops. Spoon the ice cream into an airtight, freezerproof container and loosely stir the remaining fig jam through the ice cream. Cover and freeze for at least 4 hours, or preferably overnight, until firm. Remove and allow the ice cream to soften for 10 minutes before scooping.

STRAWBERRY AND BUTTERMILK ICE CREAM

Whether you're picking your own or simply grabbing a punnet from a shop, whip up this recipe in the summer season while berries are in their prime. The tart, rich buttermilk and lemon tease out the flavour of the juicy strawberries. The riper the strawberries, the more inviting the colour.

SERVES 6-8
MAKES 1.2 LITRES (2 PINTS)

STRAWBERRY COMPÔTE

300g (10½oz) strawberries, hulled and quartered

50g (1¾oz) caster sugar

1 tablespoon fresh lemon juice

ICE CREAM BASE

400ml (14fl oz) double cream

125g (4½oz) caster sugar

Zest of 1 unwaxed lemon

1 teaspoon vanilla bean paste

300ml (½ pint) buttermilk

Tip the prepared strawberries into a bowl and sprinkle over the sugar and lemon juice. Gently mix, cover and leave to macerate for 2 hours.

Meanwhile, make the ice cream. Put the cream, sugar, lemon zest and vanilla in a saucepan over a low heat. Bring to a gentle simmer, stirring until the sugar dissolves, roughly 6–8 minutes. Remove the pan from the heat and leave to cool completely (this will take at least an hour). Pass the mixture through a sieve into a bowl to strain out the lemon zest. Stir through the buttermilk.

Using a masher, gently squash the strawberries into a rough purée. Stir three-quarters of the purée into the ice-cream mixture, setting the remaining quarter aside for later. The mixture will turn a pale pink.

Churn in an ice-cream machine following the manufacturer's instructions. Five minutes before the ice cream has a soft set, remove the lid and add the reserved strawberries. Replace the lid and allow them to mix in completely. Spoon the soft ice cream into an airtight, freezerproof container. Cover and put in the freezer for at least 4 hours, or preferably overnight, until firm.

Remove from the freezer and allow the ice cream to soften for 5–10 minutes before scooping.

DARK CHOCOLATE ICE CREAM

The secret behind this silky smooth recipe is using a giant slab of dark chocolate, melted by the warmth of whole milk for added richness. Use chocolate with a high cocoa content (70% will do the trick) and a flavour note you really love.

SERVES 6–8
MAKES 1.2 LITRES (2 PINTS)

200g (7oz) dark (minimum 70% cocoa solids) chocolate, broken into 2–3cm (³/₄–1¹/₄in) chunks

150g (5¹/₂oz) granulated sugar

275ml (9¹/₂fl oz) whole milk

450ml (16fl oz) double cream

1 teaspoon vanilla bean paste

Put the chocolate and sugar into the bowl of a food processor and pulse until finely chopped and the mixture resembles chocolate sugar. Pour the milk, cream and vanilla into a saucepan and gently heat until bubbles appear at the edges. Remove from the heat just before the mixture reaches a simmer. With the motor running, add the hot creamy milk to the food processor and blend until silky smooth. Pour into a jug or bowl and cover. Set aside in the refrigerator to cool for 1–2 hours.

Pour into an ice-cream machine and churn to a soft set following the manufacturer's instructions, or until the blade stops. Spoon the ice cream into an airtight, freezerproof container. Cover and freeze for at least 4 hours, or preferably overnight, until firm. Remove and allow the ice cream to soften for 5–10 minutes before scooping.

CRÈME FRAÎCHE ICE CREAM

You can whip up this ice cream in 5 minutes and you don't need an ice-cream machine. We created this recipe following a request from several chefs who were looking for a sharper accompaniment to sweet puddings. Crème fraîche lends a satisfyingly sour, lemony note, so pair this one with our Classic Sticky Toffee Pudding (page 118) to offset its sweetness. Look out for its cameo appearance in our Vanilla Arctic Roll recipe, too (page 88).

SERVES 6
MAKES 1 LITRE (1³/₄ PINTS)

500g (1lb 2oz) full-fat crème fraîche

200g (7oz) mascarpone

200g (7oz) icing sugar

Juice of 1 lemon (you need 3 tablespoons)

Place the crème fraîche and mascarpone into a large bowl and stir to combine.

Sift over the icing sugar and again stir for 1–2 minutes until the icing sugar has dissolved. Stir through the lemon juice.

Spoon the mixture into an airtight, freezerproof container and freeze for at least 4 hours, or preferably overnight, until firm.

Remove from the freezer and allow the ice cream to soften for 10–15 minutes before scooping.

BLACKBERRY ICE CREAM

The intense hue of this berry based scoop is a treat for your eyes and taste buds alike. This is a delicious and useful recipe for using up blackberries that have been picked and are getting a bit squidgy. We use this ice cream in our Black and Blue Freakshake on page 126.

SERVES 6
MAKES 1 LITRE (1¾ PINTS)

200g (7oz) blackberries
125g (4½oz) golden caster sugar
350ml (12fl oz) double cream
200ml (7fl oz) whole milk
A pinch of salt
5 large egg yolks

TOP TIP

We have a cheeky variation on this recipe where we stir grated dark chocolate through before freezing – the bitterness of the chocolate perfectly brings out the sweetness of the berries.

Put the blackberries into a small bowl and, using a masher, lightly crush with 25g (1oz) of the sugar. Set aside.

Pour the cream and milk into a small saucepan and warm over a gentle heat, for 2–3 minutes, until tepid. Remove from the heat and set aside.

Meanwhile, with a wooden spoon, beat the salt, egg yolks and the remainder of the sugar in a large mixing bowl until well combined.

Slowly pour the warmed cream mixture into the sugared yolks and stir with a wooden spoon until combined. Return the lot to a clean saucepan and cook over a gentle heat, stirring continuously, for up to 10 minutes. The mixture will eventually thicken to a custard consistency, just thick enough to coat the back of a wooden spoon. At this point, remove from the heat and transfer to a clean bowl (this prevents any further cooking). Set aside to cool for an hour before combining with the crushed blackberries. Pour into an ice-cream machine and churn to a soft set following the manufacturer's instructions, or until the blade stops.

Spoon into an airtight, freezerproof container and put in the freezer for a further 4 hours or overnight, until firm. Remove from the freezer and allow the ice cream to soften for 5–10 minutes before scooping.

 TIP If your custard mix is at all lumpy, simply sieve the mix when you take it off the heat.

SALTED CARAMEL ICE CREAM

Salty, sweet and incredibly creamy, this is Jude's signature flavour. It's also our supermarket bestseller right across the country. Now we're giving you the chance to make it yourself at home. Our top tip for making this ice cream? Allow the caramel to become really dark in colour as it simmers in your saucepan. A lighter caramel makes for a sweet scoop, but the darker the caramel the deeper the flavour note. Use sea salt for a real artisan touch.

SERVES 6–8
MAKES 1.2 LITRES (2 PINTS)

150g (5½oz) caster sugar

4 tablespoons water (60ml)

450ml (16fl oz) double cream

220ml (scant 8fl oz) whole milk

1 teaspoon vanilla bean paste

½ teaspoon sea salt flakes

Put the sugar and water into a heavy-based medium saucepan (not non-stick as you need to be able to see the colour of the caramel) and place over a low heat to melt very gently. Stir occasionally, and keep a bowl of water and a heatproof pastry brush handy so you can brush down the sides of the pan with water to dislodge any sugar crystals that stick.

Meanwhile, gently warm the cream and milk in another medium saucepan.

Once the sugar has completely dissolved, turn up the heat and boil rapidly without stirring until the syrup turns a rich caramel brown. Remove the pan from the heat, cover your hand with an oven glove (the mixture will splutter and could burn your bare skin) and slowly pour in the warmed cream and milk. Return the pan to a low heat and whisk with a wire hand whisk for about a minute, until very smooth and thick. Stir in the vanilla bean paste and sea salt flakes. Pour into a heatproof bowl, then cover and allow to cool for 45 minutes.

Pour into an ice-cream machine and churn to a soft set following the manufacturer's instructions, or until the blade stops. Spoon the soft ice cream into an airtight, freezerproof container. Cover and put in the freezer for at least 4 hours, or preferably overnight, until firm.

Remove from the freezer and allow the ice cream to soften for 5–10 minutes before scooping.

MALTED MILK ICE CREAM
WITH CHOCOLATE CARAMEL

If you're a malted milk kind of person, this is like a hug in a tub. It's a lovely, smooth, delicate ice cream that works all year round. We love to go for it with chocolate sauce and Maltesers – scattering them on top as well as stirring them into the ice cream for extra texture and crunch in every bite. If you've got any leftover scoops – unlikely, but bear with us – whizz them into a milkshake for a sweet 'n' tasty treat.

SERVES 4
MAKES 750ML (1⅓ PINTS)

60g (2¼oz) malted milk powder (Horlicks is good)

100ml (3½fl oz) whole milk, warmed

150g (5½oz) icing sugar, sifted

500ml (18fl oz) double cream

CHOCOLATE CARAMEL

50g (1¾oz) unsalted butter

50g (1¾oz) soft light brown sugar

60ml (2¼fl oz) double cream

80g Maltesers, lightly crushed, plus extra to serve

40g (1½oz) dark chocolate (minimum 70% cocoa solids), roughly chopped

To make the chocolate caramel, put the butter, brown sugar, double cream and dark chocolate into a small saucepan over a low heat to melt gently. Increase the heat and let it bubble for 2–3 minutes, stirring continuously. Remove from the heat and allow to cool completely.

Tip the malted milk powder into a medium bowl and pour over the warm milk. Stir until the powder dissolves and has formed a smooth, thick paste. Sift over the icing sugar and beat with a wooden spoon until dissolved. Allow to cool for 4–5 minutes before pouring in the cream. Using an electric handheld whisk, beat for 4–5 minutes until thick and voluminous with soft peaks and the whisk leaves a trail on the surface.

Pour the ice cream base into a freezerproof container, swirl through the cool chocolate caramel sauce and the Maltesers. Cover and freeze for at least 4 hours but preferably overnight, until firm.

Remove the ice cream from the freezer and allow to soften for 10 minutes before scooping. Serve scattered with a few extra crushed Maltesers.

TAHINI AND CARDAMOM ICE CREAM

Fragrant and exotic, tahini and cardamom are a perfect match. Tahini, made from sesame seeds, is now easy to come by in the supermarket, but we recommend paying a visit to a Middle Eastern shop for a paste that is really loaded with flavour. A superior taste will really shine through and help your ice cream pack even more of a punch. Ground cardamom is harder to find than the whole pods, so we suggest making your own by crushing the seeds using a pestle and mortar. This means the flavour will be extra fresh and intense.

SERVES 6
MAKES 1 LITRE (1¾ PINTS)

4 cardamom pods

300ml (½ pint) whole milk

300ml (½ pint) double cream

150g (5½oz) tahini

125ml (4fl oz) agave syrup

3 medium egg yolks

Toasted sesame seeds, to serve

Bruise the cardamom pods hard enough to split them and shake their black seeds and the papery cases into a mortar. Crush for a minute or so using a pestle and put into a saucepan along with the milk and cream. Warm over a gentle heat for 5 minutes or so, until the creamy milk just begins to simmer. Remove from the heat. Let the mixture sit for 5 minutes or so to infuse, then strain.

Meanwhile, put the tahini and agave syrup into a medium saucepan and warm over a medium heat, stirring continuously, for about 4–5 minutes until the mixture comes together and begins to simmer. Remove from the heat and pour the cardamom milk into the tahini, stirring all the while.

Put the egg yolks into a large bowl and pour over the tahini milk mixture, slowly at first, stirring with a wooden spoon. Return the lot to a clean saucepan and cook over a gentle heat, stirring continuously, for up to 10 minutes. The mixture will eventually thicken to custard consistency, just thick enough to coat the back of the wooden spoon. At this point, remove from the heat and transfer to a clean bowl (this prevents any further cooking). Set aside to cool for 1–2 hours.

Pour into an ice-cream machine and churn to a soft set following the manufacturer's instructions, or until the blade stops. Spoon the soft ice cream into an airtight, freezerproof container and freeze for at least 4 hours, or preferably overnight, until firm. Remove from the freezer and allow the ice cream to soften for 5–10 minutes before scooping. Serve scattered with toasted sesame seeds.

MATCHA ICE CREAM WITH BLACK SESAME BRITTLE

Earthy and slightly bitter, matcha's vibrant green colour makes for a cheerful-looking ice cream. It's said to be extremely high in healthy antioxidants, too, but we're most excited by its delicious flavour. Serve alongside a snap of black sesame brittle for a sophisticated dessert.

SERVES 6
MAKES 1 LITRE (1¾ PINTS)

ICE CREAM

220ml (scant 8fl oz) whole milk

150g (5½oz) granulated sugar

450ml (16fl oz) double cream

1 teaspoon vanilla extract

3 teaspoons matcha powder

BRITTLE

10g (¼oz) unsalted butter

100g (3½oz) granulated sugar

2 teaspoons cold water

100g (3½oz) golden syrup

75g (2¾oz) black sesame seeds

50g (1¾oz) white sesame seeds

Pour the milk and sugar into a medium bowl and stir, with a wooden spoon, until the sugar has dissolved, about 5–6 minutes. Add the double cream and vanilla. In a small bowl, combine the matcha with 1 tablespoon of the milk mixture to make a smooth paste. Add another 2 tablespoons milk mixture gradually to the paste, stirring constantly. Add the matcha to the rest of the milk mixture, stir until combined and set aside in the refrigerator for 4 hours, or preferably overnight, to allow the flavours to develop.

Pour into an ice-cream machine and churn to a soft set following the manufacturer's instructions, or until the blade stops. Spoon the soft ice cream into an airtight, freezerproof container. Cover and put in the freezer for at least 4 hours, or preferably overnight, until firm.

Meanwhile, make the brittle. Line a baking sheet with baking parchment and set a small bowl of ice-cold water on the work surface, to test if the brittle is at the correct stage. Put the butter, sugar, water and golden syrup in a medium saucepan over a medium-high heat and bring to the boil. Cook, gently swirling the pan, until the sugar begins to melt and turn golden, and the temperature reaches 150°C (300°F), hard crack stage. Test for doneness by dropping a small teaspoon of the mixture into the bowl of ice-cold water – if it forms a soft, squidgy ball, it's ready, if it doesn't, cook for another minute and re-test the mixture until this point is reached. Stir in the sesame seeds and cook for 2–3 minutes until the caramel comes back up to temperature. Test the mixture again at this point, dropping a small spoonful into fresh ice-cold water – again, you are looking for a soft, squidgy ball. Pour the brittle onto the lined baking sheet and leave to set for 20 minutes, then lift out, peel off the paper and snap into pieces.

Remove the matcha ice cream from the freezer and allow to soften for a few minutes. Serve with scattered brittle pieces on top.

ONE ICE CREAM – FOUR SEASONS

This no-churn vanilla base can be made in moments. The secret star of the show is the thick, sweet condensed milk. It doesn't freeze hard, which makes for easy scooping. Once you know how to make your vanilla base, the possibilities never end. Here we've suggested four ideas to get you going – one for each season. The idea is to reach for fresh ingredients when they're at their very best.

SERVES 5–6
MAKES 750ML (1⅓ PINTS)

VANILLA ICE-CREAM BASE

½ x 397g (14oz) can condensed milk

600ml (20fl oz) double cream

1 teaspoon vanilla extract

SPRING: RHUBARB

300g (10½oz) pink rhubarb, trimmed and cut into 2.5cm (1in) lengths

60g (2¼oz) golden caster sugar

SUMMER: ELDERFLOWER

3 tablespoons elderflower cordial

1 teaspoon vanilla bean paste

AUTUMN: TURMERIC

35g (1¼oz) fresh turmeric, peeled and finely grated

WINTER: BLOOD ORANGE

100ml (3½fl oz) blood orange juice (you will need about 3 oranges)

For the ice-cream base, pour the condensed milk, double cream and vanilla into a large bowl and beat with an electric whisk for 3–4 minutes, or until the mixture becomes thick and stiff. This is the moment to stir in any additions (for the rhubarb compôte, see below).

Spoon the ice-cream base into an airtight, freezerproof container and freeze for at least 4 hours, or preferably overnight, until firm. Remove from the freezer and allow the ice cream to soften for 5–10 minutes before scooping.

For the rhubarb compôte, put the rhubarb and sugar in a small saucepan over a medium heat and slowly bring to a simmer. Turn down the heat and cook for about 12 minutes until the rhubarb is soft and cooked. Allow the compôte to cool completely then stir three-quarters into the ice cream and spoon the remaining compôte over the top of the ice cream mixture before freezing.

SUMMER FRUIT SWIRL LOLLIES

These pops are perfect for children as they're not too sweet, so you can happily hand these out when the sun is shining. We've layered ours up in the ice cream mould, but be free to unleash your inner artist and go your own way. You could marble the ingredients in the mould, or mix them all together entirely before you pour them in.

MAKES 10 X 90ML (3¼FL OZ) LOLLIES

150g (5½oz) strawberries, hulled and halved

150g (5½oz) raspberries

400g (14oz) full-fat natural yogurt

1 tablespoon clear honey

100g (3½oz) milk chocolate, melted, to serve

YOU WILL NEED

10 x 90ml (3¼fl oz) ice-lolly moulds and sticks

Start with the berry purée. Put the strawberries and the raspberries in a blender and purée into a smooth, thick paste. Set aside.

Sweeten the yogurt by mixing it with the honey in a mixing bowl.

Alternate small teaspoons of the purée and the yogurt mixture into the lolly moulds until each is full. Place in the freezer until the lollies are part frozen then insert sticks into the moulds and freeze upright for at least 4 hours or preferably overnight, until firm.

Remove the lollies from the freezer, dip the moulds in hot water, gently pull the lollies out of the mould, then, working quickly, drizzle with the melted milk chocolate. Serve straight away.

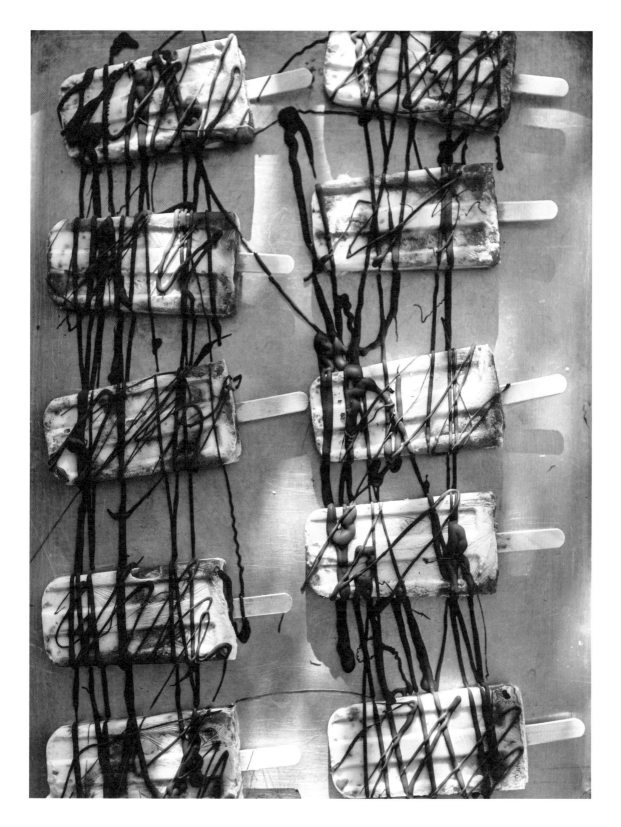

SCOOPS: DAIRY & VEGAN ➤ | 35

BEETROOT AND GINGER ICE CREAM

This combination may be unexpected, but it's a winner. Beetroot gives this ice cream its vibrant, look-at-me colour. The vegetable's natural depth of flavour balances the fiery ginger perfectly. Do wear gloves and protect your kitchen surfaces as you peel beetroot, because it has a habit of turning everything deep pink. And one tasty hint – serve with Glossy Hot Chocolate Sauce (page 154).

SERVES 8
MAKES 1.3 LITRES (2¼ PINTS)

350g (12oz) beetroot (about 3), trimmed and peeled into 3–4cm (1¼–1½in) chunks

50g (1¾oz) fresh ginger, peeled and quartered

1 tablespoon fresh lemon juice

1–2 tablespoons cold water

170ml (scant 6fl oz) whole milk

150g (5½oz) granulated sugar

500ml (18fl oz) double cream

2 teaspoons vanilla bean paste

Put the beetroot and ginger into a blender or juicer along with the lemon juice and 1 tablespoon of water. Blend until smooth, adding the second tablespoon of water if needed to get everything moving. Strain the juice through a sieve into a waiting jug. Press the pulp with the back of the spoon to ensure as much juice is extracted as possible – you want roughly 175ml (6fl oz).

Pour the milk and sugar into a medium bowl and stir for 2–3 minutes until the sugar has dissolved. Add the double cream, vanilla paste and the beetroot and ginger juice. Stir until combined, then set aside in the refrigerator for an hour or so to allow the flavours to develop.

Pour into an ice-cream machine and churn to a soft set following the manufacturer's instructions, or until the blade stops. Spoon the soft ice cream into an airtight, freezerproof container and put in the freezer for at least 4 hours, or preferably overnight, until firm. Remove from the freezer and allow the ice cream to soften for a few minutes before scooping.

 TIP When peeling the ginger, use a teaspoon. Ginger skin is papery and delicate and can easily be scraped away with a small spoon.

FLAT WHITE COFFEE ICE CREAM

We're a family of coffee lovers, so we just had to include this intense and heady ice cream. It's smooth, it's rich, and it's dreamy. It's also the ultimate end to a dinner party. Jude's Flat White Coffee Ice Cream has bagged a Great Taste award and remains one of our personal all-time favourites. We've recreated the flavour here so you can make the magic at home for friends and family.

SERVES 4–5
MAKES 700ML (1¼ PINTS)

75ml (2½fl oz) strong coffee
   (2 generous shots)

175g (6oz) icing sugar

500ml (18fl oz) double cream

Pinch of ground coffee, to serve

Make the coffee using a cafetière and pour into a large bowl. Add the icing sugar and whisk until dissolved. Allow to cool for 5 minutes before pouring in the double cream. Using an electric handheld whisk, beat for 4–5 minutes until thick, voluminous soft peaks form and the whisk leaves a trail over the surface.

Spoon the ice-cream base into an airtight, freezerproof container and put in the freezer for at least 4 hours, or preferably overnight, until firm. Remove from the freezer and allow the ice cream to soften for 5–10 minutes before scooping. Serve with a sprinkling of ground coffee on top.

EARL GREY ICE CREAM

This refreshing summer ice cream is perfect for those moments when you fancy a little something, but it's too hot for a cuppa. Earl Grey tea has delicious fruity and slightly smoky notes and if you're a tea lover, your palate will recognize it from the very first spoonful. Use loose leaf tea for a really powerful flavour. The longer the tea is brewed, the stronger the taste, so put your feet up and take your time.

SERVES 6–8
MAKES 1.2 LITRES (2 PINTS)

30g (1oz) Earl Grey tea leaves
  or 6 Earl Grey teabags

200ml (7fl oz) boiling water

4 medium egg yolks

100g (3½oz) golden caster sugar

200ml (7fl oz) whole milk

400ml (14fl oz) double cream

A pinch of fine salt

First, steep the tea for the ice-cream base. Put the tea leaves or bags in a small bowl and pour over the boiling water. Leave the tea to stew until cold and then remove the leaves or bags, either by passing the liquid through a sieve or gently squeezing the tea bags to extract the liquid.

Using a wooden spoon, beat the egg yolks and sugar together in a large mixing bowl for 2–3 minutes until light and uniform. Stir through the cold tea.

Pour the milk, cream and salt into a medium saucepan and gently warm over a low heat. Slowly pour the warm milky mixture onto the yolks mixture and continue to beat until everything is combined. Return the lot to a clean saucepan and cook over a gentle heat, stirring continuously, for up to 10 minutes. The mixture will eventually thicken to a custard consistency, just thick enough to coat the back of the wooden spoon. At this point, remove from the heat and transfer to a clean bowl (this prevents any further cooking). Set aside to cool for an hour.

Pour into an ice-cream machine and churn to a soft set following the manufacturer's instructions, or until the blade stops. Spoon the soft ice cream into an airtight, freezerproof container and put in the freezer for at least 4 hours, or preferably overnight, until firm. Remove from the freezer and allow the ice cream to soften for 5–10 minutes before scooping.

MOCHA VIETNAMESE-STYLE LOLLIES

Order a coffee in Vietnam and you'll find a generous spoonful of condensed milk sitting at the bottom of your glass. It ups the indulgence factor and lends a creamy texture. We've taken that idea and turned it into a moreish and rather grown-up lolly. Enjoy these treats on a long, lazy summer afternoon, or serve as an informal dessert that will get everyone talking – in between licks, of course.

MAKES 8 X 60ML (2¼FL OZ) LOLLIES

50g (1¾oz) dark chocolate (minimum 70% cocoa solids)

300ml (½ pint) hot, strong coffee

120ml (4fl oz) condensed milk

YOU WILL NEED

8 x 60ml (2¼fl oz) ice-lolly moulds and sticks

Using the fine side of a box grater, grate the dark chocolate into a small bowl and pour over the hot coffee. Stir until melted and add the condensed milk. Mix until the colour is an even milky brown, then pour into the moulds.

Put in the freezer upright or an hour or so before poking an ice-lolly stick into each mould. Continue to freeze for a further 3 hours or, preferably, overnight until solid.

Remove the lollies from the freezer, dip the moulds briefly in hot water, then gently pull the lollies out of the moulds and serve straight away.

VEGAN COCONUT ICE CREAM

This vegan ice cream is so easy to create at home. It's unexpectedly creamy, with a fresh coconut flavour that makes your mind instantly wander to tropical islands. We've used cornflour for extra smoothness and love serving it with toasted coconut flakes, which give nutty taste and texture, but if that's not your thing, simply serve it straight up.

SERVES 6
MAKES 1 LITRE (1¾ PINTS)

1 x 400g (14oz) can coconut milk

1 tablespoon cornflour

300ml (½ pint) coconut cream

175g (6oz) agave syrup
  (or honey, for a non-vegan option)

¼ teaspoon fine salt

Handful of coconut flakes,
  toasted, to serve (optional)

Combine 1 tablespoon of the coconut milk with the cornflour to make a paste. Gradually add a further 2 tablespoons of the coconut milk, stirring constantly. Pour the remaining coconut milk into a saucepan over a low heat with the coconut cream and agave syrup. Bring slowly to a simmer, then stir in the cornflour paste and salt. Bring the mixture to the boil, stirring constantly until slightly thickened, then remove from the heat. Cover the pan, cool and chill in the refrigerator overnight, or if you don't have time, for at least 2 hours.

Pour into an ice-cream machine and churn to a soft set following the manufacturer's instructions, or until the blade stops. Spoon the soft ice cream into an airtight, freezerproof container and put in the freezer for at least 4 hours, or preferably overnight, until firm. Remove from the freezer and allow the ice cream to soften for 5–10 minutes before scooping. Serve with toasted coconut flakes, if using.

VEGAN BANANA AND NUT BUTTER ICE CREAM

You'll go wild for this silky smooth, no-churn, vegan ice cream. It works brilliantly with almond or peanut butter, but feel free to use your favourite nut butter, or whichever you have lurking in the cupboard. Serve this scoop with chopped nuts and dried banana chips for a cheeky crunch.

SERVES 4
MAKES 700ML (1¼ PINTS)

4 frozen (peeled) bananas (total
  weight 375g/13oz)
175g (6oz) nut butter (almond,
  peanut or cashew)
250ml (9fl oz) almond milk
125g (4½oz) icing sugar, sifted

TO SERVE

A handful of salted peanuts, roughly
  chopped (optional)
A handful of dried banana chips
  (optional)

Chop the frozen bananas into manageable pieces, roughly 4cm (1½in) long. Put them into a food processor with the nut butter, almond milk and icing sugar. Blend to a soft, silky-smooth purée.

Spoon the ice-cream base into an airtight, freezerproof container and put in the freezer for at least 4 hours, or preferably overnight, until firm. Remove from the freezer and allow the ice cream to soften for 10 minutes before scooping.

Serve topped with chopped peanuts and banana chips, if you ilke.

INSTANT BANANA ICE CREAM

SERVES 2–3 CHILDREN

4 ripe bananas
extra flavourings (see Tip below)

Peel the bananas, cut each one into chunks and lay them on a baking sheet. Freeze overnight.

Put the frozen banana chunks in a food processor and blend until you have a soft, spoonable consistency. Spoon into bowls and serve straight away.

TIP: Try adding different flavourings to perfect a favourite: 1 teaspoon of cocoa powder, the grated zest and juice of an unwaxed lime or 1 teaspoon of peanut butter.

VEGAN DOUBLE DARK CHOCOLATE ICE CREAM

This chocolate stunner isn't for the faint-hearted. With both dark chocolate and cocoa powder in the mix, it has a deep, intense taste. Oh, and it happens to be vegan. Plenty of experimentation, tasting and refinement went into this one and it was worth the effort.

SERVES 6
MAKES 1 LITRE (1¾ PINTS)

150g (5½oz) cashews

3 tablespoons good-quality cocoa powder

150ml (¼ pint) warm water

1 tablespoon liquid pectin

300ml (½ pint) coconut cream

150g (5½oz) golden caster sugar

200g (7oz) vegan dark chocolate (minimum 70% cocoa solids), broken into 2cm (¾in) squares

2 tablespoons cornflour

Put the cashews, cocoa powder, warm water and pectin into a blender and blend on high until all is silky smooth. Pour into a large bowl and set aside.

Spoon the coconut cream into a medium saucepan and add the caster sugar and dark chocolate. Heat very gently, regularly stirring, until the sugar has dissolved and the chocolate has melted into the cream.

Measure the cornflour into a small bowl and add 2 tablespoons of the coconut-chocolate mixture into the cornflour. Stir to combine until you have a thick, soft and uniform paste. Return this paste to the mixture in the pan and continue to stir over a gentle heat for 5–7 minutes, until steam rises from the surface and the cornflour has thickened the mixture. The consistency will be that of double cream.

Pour the warm coconut and chocolate base into the cashew mixture and stir thoroughly until well combined. Cover the bowl with clingfilm and set aside to cool for about 2 hours.

Pour into an ice-cream machine and churn to a soft set following the manufacturer's instructions, or until the blade stops. Spoon the soft ice cream into an airtight, freezerproof container and put in the freezer for at least 4 hours, or preferably overnight, until firm. Remove from the freezer and allow the ice cream to soften for at least 10 minutes before scooping.

 TIP: Try pouring into a springform cake tin to freeze and then cut into slices to serve.

VEGAN PEANUT BUTTER ICE CREAM

This stunner is made with coconut cream for a lovely rich texture. Peanut butter is a true crowd-pleaser and chocolate sauce brings extra indulgence, exciting pudding fans of all ages. Drizzle the sauce at the table for a spot of food theatre.

SERVES 6
MAKES 1 LITRE (1¾ PINTS)

400ml (14fl oz) coconut milk

400ml (14fl oz) coconut cream

75g (2¾oz) golden caster sugar

75ml (2½fl oz) maple syrup

1 teaspoon vanilla extract

250g (9oz) chunky peanut butter

TO SERVE

Vegan Dark Chocolate Sauce (page 158)

Toasted peanuts, roughly chopped

Pour the coconut milk, coconut cream, sugar, maple syrup and vanilla into a saucepan and bring to a gentle simmer. Remove the saucepan from the heat and stir through the peanut butter.

Either using a stick blender or, working in batches, a stand mixer, blend the mixture until the peanut butter is thoroughly combined. Transfer the mixture to a bowl, cover and set aside to cool completely for 2 hours.

Pour into an ice-cream machine and churn to a soft set following the manufacturer's instructions, or until the blade stops. Spoon into an airtight, freezerproof container and put in the freezer for 4–6 hours.

Remove the ice cream from the freezer and allow to soften for at least 10 minutes before scooping. Serve with hot or cold chocolate sauce and a scattering of peanuts.

 TIP: The chocolate sauce will keep perfectly well for up to a week in the refrigerator. Simply reheat for a few seconds in the microwave if a hot sauce is required.

VEGAN ALMOND MILK ICE CREAM

Almonds are naturally mild and creamy, so it should come as no surprise that this is a soft, delicate ice cream. To add a touch of 'disco', we've included a chunk of marzipan, grated, and melted by the warmth of the almond milk. As it dissolves into the ice cream base, it immediately infuses its lovely rich almond notes.

SERVES 5-6
MAKES 750ML (1⅓ PINTS)

600ml (20fl oz) almond milk

1 teaspoon vanilla bean paste

140g (5oz) white marzipan

½ teaspoon powdered xanthan gum

2 teaspoons liquid pectin

150g (5½oz) icing sugar, sifted

Small handful of pistachio nibs, to serve (optional)

Gently warm the almond milk and vanilla bean paste in a medium saucepan and, just as the milk begins to simmer and steam rises from the surface, remove from the heat. Using the coarse side of a box grater, grate the marzipan into the milk and stir intermittently until the marzipan melts, roughly 5–6 minutes. If any pieces of marzipan are refusing to melt, briefly return the pan to the heat and continue to stir until they disappear.

Tip the xanthan gum into a small bowl and add 2 tablespoons of the warm almond milk mixture. Stir to combine until you have a thick, soft and uniform paste. Return this paste to the saucepan and continue to stir until dissolved. Remove from the heat. Stir in the pectin and icing sugar and again, stir until smooth and uniform. Set the mixture aside to cool for 2 hours.

Pour into an ice-cream machine and churn to a soft set following the manufacturer's instructions, or until the blade stops. Spoon the soft ice cream into an airtight, freezerproof container and put in the freezer for at least 4 hours, or preferably overnight, until firm. Remove from the freezer and allow the ice cream to soften for 5–10 minutes before scooping. Serve with pistachio nibs, if using.

RASPBERRY RIPPLE FROZEN YOGURT

A twist on traditional raspberry ripple, using Greek yogurt for a fresh, tart scoop.
Use full-fat yogurt for maximum flavour and that must-have creamy texture, because
low-fat yogurts can make for an icy dessert. We like to add a little cornflour, too,
which keeps things smooth. If raspberries aren't at their peak, a good-quality jam will
do the trick for the ripple. Simply swirl through the ice cream to taste.

SERVES 8-10
MAKES 1.5 LITRES (2 ¾ PINTS)

BERRY RIPPLE

250g (9oz) raspberries

75ml (2½fl oz) maple syrup

A squeeze of lemon juice
  (1 teaspoon)

A small pinch of fine salt

FROZEN YOGURT

200ml (7fl oz) whole milk

2 tablespoons cornflour

1kg (2lb 4oz) full-fat Greek yogurt

250g (9oz) golden caster sugar

A little lemon juice, to taste

To make the berry ripple, put the raspberries in a saucepan with the maple syrup. Heat gently, stirring occasionally, for 10–15 minutes, until the berries burst and reduce by half. Stir in the lemon juice and the salt. Set aside to cool, then chill in the refrigerator until needed.

Meanwhile, for the frozen yogurt, combine 2 tablespoons of the milk with the cornflour in a bowl and mix to make a smooth paste. Slowly stir in the remaining milk and transfer the lot to a small pan. Cook, stirring constantly, over a medium heat for 2–3 minutes until just below simmering; you'll notice steam rising from the surface and the consistency becoming thicker. Remove the pan from the heat and set aside to cool.

Scrape the yogurt into a bowl with the sugar. Stir constantly for 2–3 minutes until the sugar has dissolved and then pour in the cooled milk along with the lemon juice to taste. Stir to combine. Pour into an ice-cream machine and churn to a soft set following the manufacturer's instructions, or until the blade stops. Spoon the soft ice cream into an airtight, freezerproof container. Drizzle the raspberry ripple over the ice cream and gently mix, but not too much! It's lovely to see frozen yogurt with separate pockets of raspberry ripple.

Cover and put in the freezer for at least 4 hours, or preferably overnight, until firm. Remove from the freezer and allow the ice cream to soften for 10 minutes before scooping.

TROPICAL SMOOTHIE BOWL

Enter this healthy smoothie, bursting with goodness. It's a beautiful way
to add nutrients to your breakfast and, even better, it's ready in minutes.
Go ahead and customize the toppings to get your personal favourites in there.
This recipe also works brilliantly as a dessert.

SERVES 2

3 tablespoons toasted coconut
  flakes (optional)

1 banana, peeled, halved
  and frozen

1 papaya, peeled, deseeded,
  cut into thick slices and frozen

200ml (7fl oz) orange juice

Juice of 1 lime

TO SERVE

1 kiwi fruit, peeled and sliced

100g (3½oz) fresh raspberries,
  frozen (or use frozen)

6–8 slices of mango or papaya flesh

Zest of 1 unwaxed lime

Small handful of Granola
  (page 166)

Heat a small, dry frying pan over a medium heat and toast the
coconut shavings, if using. Fry for 1–2 minutes until the edges
begin to brown. Remove from the heat and set aside.

Put the frozen banana, frozen papaya and orange juice in a
blender and blitz to a thick, smooth consistency, scraping down
the sides with a spoon, if necessary. Stir through the lime juice
to taste.

Divide the smoothie between two bowls and decorate with
sliced kiwi fruit, frozen raspberries, mango slices and the lime
zest. Sprinkle over the granola and coconut flakes, if using.
Eat immediately.

SUMMER PEACH SORBET

This stunner couldn't be simpler. It's made of just three ingredients, with the sweet taste of fresh peaches taking centre stage. When they're in season, it's just sensational. It's sure to become a regular favourite, so why not try something new each time you make it? Experiment by using both yellow and white flesh peach varieties – each lends its own unique colour and taste.

SERVES 4
MAKES 1 LITRE (1¾ PINTS)

5 big, ripe peaches, about 750g (1lb 10oz) in weight, halved and stoned

175g (6oz) golden caster sugar

Juice of 1 lime, or extra to taste

Simply cut up the peaches, skin and all, and put into a food processor. Add the sugar and blend to a smooth, velvety pulp. Stir through the lime juice. Taste and add more lime juice if necessary – remember the flavour will dull once the ice cream is frozen.

Pour into a 1.2-litre (2-pint) airtight, freezerproof container and freeze overnight. Remove from the freezer and allow to soften for 10 minutes or so, before scooping.

WATERMELON AND STRAWBERRY GRANITA

This vibrant recipe is the ultimate summer cooler. If you've not encountered granita before, it's a frozen fruit syrup made from fresh fruit and water, blended and frozen until icy, then flaked with a fork until frozen again. In Sicily, it's common for locals to eat granita at breakfast time – we like their style. If you're giving this recipe a go, make sure you'll be at home for most of the day. You'll be making regular trips to the freezer to tend to your creation. It's best served the same day, while it's at its freshest.

SERVES 8-10
MAKES ABOUT 1.3 LITRES
(2¼ PINTS)

1 unwaxed lime

100g (3½oz) golden caster sugar

200ml (7fl oz) water, at room temperature

½ watermelon (about 1.2kg/ 2lb 12 oz) peeled, deseeded and cut into chunks (approx. 750g/ 1lb10oz flesh)

250g (9oz) strawberries, hulled and halved, plus extra to decorate, if desired

Thinly pare the rind from the lime and put it in a small saucepan with the sugar and water. Squeeze the lime juice into the pan. Bring to the boil and simmer for 6–8 minutes until the volume is reduced roughly by half to make a syrup. Remove from the heat, and set aside to cool to room temperature before removing the lime rind.

Put the cooled syrup, watermelon chunks and strawberries in the bowl of a food processor and pulse until smooth. Pour into a shallow baking dish (ceramic or metal – a metal one will freeze fastest) and spread the bright red pulp evenly. Transfer to the freezer and freeze the mixture until the edges begin to set, for about 30–35 minutes. Remove from the freezer and use a fork to scrape and break up the frozen portions. Freeze again, scraping and breaking up the granita every 20–30 minutes until it resembles fluffy shaved ice – the total time will take 2–4 hours.

Serve the granita in bowls or glasses, decorated with strawberries, if using.

MANGO AND PASSION FRUIT SORBET

Golden and glossy, the colour and texture here screams summer. Seek out the very best mangoes available. We're big fans of Alphonso mangoes, which we use in our Great Taste award-winning Mango Sorbet. Hailing from India, this variety is known for its intense sunshine hue and deep, rich flavour. They are hard to find year round so Kesar are a brilliant alternative. Serve al fresco to do this refreshing sorbet full justice.

SERVES 6
MAKES 1 LITRE (1¾ PINTS)

400g (14oz) ripe Alphonso or Kesar mango flesh, cut into rough 2–3cm (¾–1¼in) cubes (about 2 large mangoes)

200g (7oz) granulated sugar

Juice of 1 large lemon (about 4 tablespoons juice)

300ml (½ pint) fresh orange juice

Pulp from 6 passion fruits

Put the mango cubes, sugar and lemon juice into a medium bowl and leave to macerate for 2 hours. The sugar will mostly dissolve and the flavours develop.

Empty the sugary mango mixture into the bowl of a food processor and blitz to a silky, smooth consistency. Add the fresh orange juice and passion fruit pulp and stir to combine.

Pour the sorbet into an ice-cream machine and churn until the blade stops. Transfer to an airtight, freezerproof container, cover, and put in the freezer for at least 4 hours, but preferably overnight until firm. Remove from the freezer and allow the sorbet to soften for a few minutes before scooping.

 TIP: You could squeeze your own orange juice, but we find good-quality shop-bought OJ is perfect.

TART LEMON SORBET

We love three-ingredient recipes; they are so satisfyingly simple and this sorbet is an all-time favourite. It's sharp and sweet and really hits the spot. When you're shopping for the ingredients, be sure to pick up unwaxed lemons for the zingiest zest. This recipe works well when poured into a ramekin, tub or tin.

MAKES 4 X 125ML (4FL OZ) MOULDS OR 500ML (18FL OZ) SORBET

300ml (½ pint) water

175g (6oz) golden caster sugar

Zest and juice of 8 unwaxed lemons (roughly 300ml/ ½ pint juice)

Put the water, sugar and lemon zest into a saucepan and bring to a simmer, stirring to dissolve the sugar. Increase the heat to a rolling boil and cook for 2 minutes before removing from the heat. Allow to cool for a few minutes, then stir in the lemon juice. Set the syrup aside to infuse and cool completely for 2–3 hours.

Pour the syrup through a fine nylon sieve to remove the lemon zest and transfer the syrup to an ice-cream machine. Churn to a soft set, following the manufacturer's instructions, or until the blade stops. Spoon the sorbet into an airtight, freezerproof container and freeze overnight.

Remove the container from the freezer 10 minutes before scooping.

ORANGE LOLLIES
ONLY 2 INGREDIENTS

Fresh, simple and honest. These delightful licks are perfect for rustling up
when you have a glut of oranges or simply to satisfy a hankering for a refreshing
pick-me-up. As the name would suggest this recipe requires just two ingredients:
fresh oranges and a squeeze of lime to bring these treats to life.

**MAKES 4 X 85ML (3FL OZ)
ICE LOLLIES**

Juice of 5–6 large oranges
  (roughly 300ml/½ pint)

A squeeze of fresh lime juice

YOU WILL NEED

4 x 85ml (3fl oz) ice-lolly
  moulds and sticks

Mix the fresh orange juice with a squeeze of fresh lime, tasting
and adjusting to your liking. Pour into the lolly moulds until each
one is three-quarters full. Put the moulds in the freezer upright
for an hour or so before poking an ice-lolly stick into each mould.
Continue to freeze for a further 3 hours, or preferably, overnight,
until solid.

Remove the moulds from the freezer and, working quickly, dip
the moulds briefly into hot water, then gently pull the lollies out
of the moulds and serve straight away.

CHAPTER 2

ICE CREAM DESSERTS

In our years of working closely with celebrated chefs, we've learned that ice cream is so much more than an excellent stand-alone dessert. Magical things can happen when you combine your favourite scoop with other ingredients to make unique and inventive puddings. This chapter is full of sensational numbers, including our Stacked Ice Cream Cheesecake (page 94) and a truly decadent Celebration Cake (page 70). Bring on the wow factor! You'll find lots of fun ideas for making desserts special. We've got Dark Chocolate and Fresh Mint Baked Alaska (page 83) and a spectacular Frozen Eton Mess (page 93). Whether you're an A* baker, an enthusiastic beginner or just an ice cream fan in search of your fix, there's plenty here to experiment with.

CELEBRATION CAKE
CRÈME FRAÎCHE AND CHOCOLATE ICE CREAM CAKE

If you're having people over, make this in advance, then casually whip it out of the freezer to wow (and delight) your guests. More is more with this extravaganza, so go crazy and serve it with sparklers, sprinkles or any of your favourite decorations.

SERVES 15
MAKES A 20CM (8IN) CAKE

BROWNIES
1 quantity of Brownies (page 110)

ICE CREAM
200g (7oz) mascarpone
500g (1lb 2oz) full-fat crème fraîche
200g (7oz) icing sugar
Juice of 1 lemon (you need 3 tablespoons)

FUDGE SAUCE
100ml (3½fl oz) double cream
100g (3½oz) condensed milk
100g (3½oz) dark chocolate (minimum 70% cocoa solids), roughly chopped

TO SERVE
4 scoops ice cream
1 ice-cream cone
Sprinkles
Sparklers

YOU WILL NEED
2 loose-based 20cm (8in) round cake tins, one with sides roughly 10cm (4in) high

Preheat the oven to 180°C/fan 160°C/gas mark 4. Line 2 x 20cm (8in) round cake tins with baking parchment.

Follow the brownie recipe on page 110, but pour the mixture into the two lined cake tins (one has to be deeper to cope with the ice cream and the second brownie layer going on top). Reduce the cooking time for the brownie mixture by 5 minutes. Set aside to cool in the tins.

Next, make the ice cream. Scrape the crème fraîche and mascarpone into a large bowl and stir to combine. Sift over the icing sugar and again stir for 1–2 minutes until the icing sugar has dissolved. Stir through the lemon juice. Pour into an ice-cream machine and churn to a soft set following the manufacturer's instructions, or until the blade stops.

Spoon the soft ice cream on top of the cooled brownie in the high-sided cake tin and transfer to the freezer to set for 4 hours.

Meanwhile, make the chocolate fudge sauce. This is an easy one: simply put all the ingredients in a medium pan and warm over a gentle heat, until melted, stirring regularly. Set aside until ready to use.

Once the ice-cream layer is frozen, spoon over 2–3 tablespoons of the chocolate fudge sauce and slot the second brownie disc on the top. Return to the freezer for at least an hour so the whole thing comes together.

Just before serving, remove the tin from the freezer and, with the help of a round-bladed knife, remove the cake from the tin. Spoon over the remaining fudge sauce and decorate with ice cream, an ice-cream cone, sprinkles and sparklers. Serve straight away.

DARK CHOCOLATE AND VANILLA ROULADE

This beautiful pudding is one that can be made in advance, so you can relax and enjoy whatever celebrations you're planning. If it collapses, don't worry, it all adds to the authentic look! Seek out a good-quality chocolate – it makes all the difference.

SERVES 8

ROULADE

Vegetable oil, for greasing

175g (6oz) dark chocolate (minimum 70% cocoa solids), broken up

5 medium eggs, separated

225g (8oz) golden caster sugar, plus extra for dusting

FILLING

½ quantity soft or 500g (1lb 2oz) Vanilla Ice Cream

Preheat the oven to 200°C/fan 180°C/gas mark 6. Grease a 33 x 23cm (13 x 9in) Swiss roll tin and line with baking parchment.

For the filling, place a large piece of baking parchment on the work surface and dollop the ice cream along its centre. Using the parchment as a guide, shape your frozen ice cream into a long log shape, the length of the Swiss roll tin, and roughly 10cm (4in) in diameter. Wrap in clingfilm and return to the freezer.

Melt the chocolate in a heatproof bowl set over a saucepan of simmering water, being careful that the base of the bowl doesn't touch the water. Stir until smooth, then set aside.

In a large, clean bowl, whisk together the egg yolks and all but 1 tablespoon of the sugar until pale and thick. Mix in the melted chocolate and 1 tablespoon of hot water, stirring until smooth.

In another large, clean bowl, whisk the egg whites until stiff, then whisk in the remaining tablespoon of sugar. Lightly fold into the chocolate mixture using a large metal spoon. Spoon the batter into the prepared tin, spread it evenly, and bake for 15–20 minutes until risen and springy to the touch. Remove the roulade from the oven, cover it, still in its tin, with a sheet of baking parchment and a damp tea towel. Leave for 15 minutes, then take off the tea towel and leave in the tin until completely cold.

Place a piece of baking parchment on the work surface and dust it with caster sugar. Turn out the roulade onto the parchment. Remove the ice cream log from the freezer, unwrap and place in the centre of the roulade. With the long side of the roulade towards you, and using the paper to help, roll up the roulade. Wrap in clingfilm and parchment paper and return to the freezer until needed. When ready to serve, remove the roulade from the freezer, unwrap and allow to sit for 3–4 minutes before slicing and serving.

GINGER AND PECAN MUFFIN-COOKIES

Unless you stow away these muffin-cookies in a high cupboard, they'll disappear in an instant. But who can blame little paws when these treats are so delicious? Think dense, gooey cookie dough baked in muffin tins. These are perfect just as they are, and all the more impressive if you serve them fresh from the oven with a scoop of melting ice cream.

MAKES 12

120g (4¼oz) butter, softened

75g (2¾oz) soft light brown sugar

75g (2¾oz) golden caster sugar

1 medium egg

1 teaspoon vanilla extract

180g (6¼oz) plain flour

½ teaspoon bicarbonate of soda

1 teaspoon ground ginger

60g (2¼oz) pecan nuts, finely chopped

A pinch of fine salt

TO SERVE

Ice cream of choice

Preheat the oven to 180°C/fan 160°C/gas mark 4 and lightly grease a 12-hole muffin tin with a little of the butter (although if you use a good-quality, non-stick tin, no greasing is necessary).

Cream the butter and sugars together in a bowl until light and fluffy. Add the egg and vanilla and stir to combine. Stir in the flour, bicarbonate of soda, ginger, chopped pecans and salt.

Divide the mixture between the muffin holes and bake for 10–12 minutes or until just firm at the edges but soft in the middle – the muffins will continue to firm up as they cool. Remove from the oven and leave in the tins to cool for at least 10 minutes before turning out and serving warm, with a scoop of ice cream sat in the centre.

LEMON MERINGUE
ICE CREAM PIE

Italian meringue atop a tart, citrusy, creamy filling: what could be more glorious?
Being the first to slice into this beauty is a true honour, so consider making it
as a modern, alternative birthday cake for the meringue fan in your life. You
can even pop white candles on top, for a chic minimalist look.

SERVES 10
MAKES A 24CM (9½IN) PIE

300g (10½oz) shortbread biscuits

75g (2¾oz) butter, melted

1 x 397g (14oz) can condensed milk

50g (1¾oz) caster sugar

4 large egg yolks (whites reserved
  for the meringue)

Zest and juice of 3 unwaxed
  lemons (about 125ml/4fl oz juice)

Zest and juice of 1 unwaxed lime
  (approx. 40ml/1½fl oz)

300ml (½ pint) whipping cream

MERINGUE

200g (7oz) caster sugar

75ml (2½fl oz) water

4 large egg whites

Line the base and sides of a 24cm (9½in) springform tin with baking parchment. Put the biscuits in a food processor and blitz to a fine crumb. Add the melted butter and continue to pulse until the mixture comes together and has the consistency of damp sand. Spoon the crumbs into the lined tin, press firmly in an even layer and put in the refrigerator for 40 minutes to firm up.

Put the condensed milk, sugar, egg yolks, the lemon and lime zests and juices into a large bowl and set over a saucepan of gently simmering water. Heat the mixture for 8–10 minutes, stirring all the time with a wooden spoon. The yolks will cook in the warmth, but be careful not to overheat and scramble them. Remove from the heat and set aside to cool for 10 minutes. Strain to remove the zest and any strands of egg. In a separate large bowl, whip the cream to soft peaks. Pour in the citrus mixture and carefully fold together, trying not to lose the volume of the cream. Pour the mixture over the cooled biscuit base and freeze overnight.

For the meringue, put the sugar and water into a heavy-based saucepan and bring to the boil, stirring occasionally. Keep a bowl of water and a heatproof pastry brush handy so you can brush down the sides of the pan with water to dislodge any sugar crystals that stick. The syrup is ready when it reaches 115°C (240°F) on a sugar thermometer or when a little dropped into a glass of cold water forms a firm ball. Remove from the heat.

Meanwhile, whisk the egg whites to stiff peaks using an electric whisk. Working as fast as possible, pour the hot syrup onto the whites in three stages, whisking after each addition. Keep whisking until the mixture is cool. The meringue should be stiff and shiny.

Remove the base from the freezer, unmould and dollop the meringue over the pie. Flash under a hot grill for 2–3 minutes or brown using a cook's blowtorch just before serving.

WHITE CHOCOLATE AND NECTARINE SEMI-FREDDO

This beautiful summer dessert is seriously easy to make. It's a throw-it-all-in affair. Do chop the nectarines up small. The fruit freezes hard, so you just want little pieces mixed into the ice cream, rather than great chunks. We've set ours in a bundt tin, but this pudding will set happily into any shape.

SERVES 10
MAKES A 26CM (10½IN) CAKE

150g (5½oz) white chocolate, broken into pieces

2 ripe nectarines, halved, stoned and roughly chopped

300ml (½ pint) double cream

1 x 397g (14oz) can condensed milk

150g (5½oz) Greek yogurt

1 teaspoon vanilla bean paste

2 large meringues (see page 163), crushed

MACERATED NECTARINES

3 ripe nectarines, halved, stoned and finely sliced

40g (1½oz) golden caster sugar

Line a 26cm (10½in) ring mould with clingfilm, allowing a 5cm (2in) overhang. Melt 100g (3½oz) of the white chocolate in a bain marie over a low heat, stirring constantly to prevent burning. Remove the chocolate from the heat and allow to cool slightly. Chop the remaining 50g (1¾oz) white chocolate into small chunks and set aside.

Put the chopped nectarines into a small bowl and, using a masher, gently mush to a thick pulp. A few visible pieces are lovely, so there's no need to purée it completely.

Put the cream, condensed milk, yogurt and vanilla bean paste in a large bowl and use electric handheld beaters to whisk until soft peaks form. Don't overbeat – you are looking for a thick and aerated consistency. Stir through the cooled melted white chocolate.

Using a large metal spoon, gently fold the chopped white chocolate, mashed nectarines and crushed meringues into the cream mixture. Pour the mixture into the lined ring mould.

Bring the overhanging clingfilm over the mixture to cover the top of the semi-freddo, then place in the freezer for 8 hours or overnight.

An hour before serving, make the macerated nectarines by simply combining the nectarine slices and sugar in a small bowl.

Turn out the semi-freddo onto a board or plate and peel away the clingfilm. Serve in slices, with the macerated nectarines alongside.

COCOA AND ALMOND MILK ICE CREAM SANDWICHES

A heavenly biscuit recipe and one that's easy to make. If you didn't have to wait for these to cool, they'd be on your plate in 20 minutes flat. You'll love the deep, heavy cocoa flavour, as well as the dark decadent look. These biscuits are gluten-free, too.

MAKES 10

3 medium egg whites

250g (9oz) icing sugar

1 teaspoon instant coffee granules

A pinch of fine salt

85g (3oz) good-quality cocoa powder

TO SERVE

10 scoops vegan Almond Milk Ice Cream (page 53)

Preheat the oven to 180°C/fan 160°C/gas mark 4. Line two large baking sheets with baking parchment.

Put the egg whites, icing sugar, ground coffee, salt and cocoa powder in a large bowl and, using a wooden spoon, mix for 1–2 minutes until uniform and smooth.

Spoon 20 scant tablespoons of the mixture onto the prepared baking sheets – the biscuits will spread, so leave 5cm (2in) space around each. Bake for 10–12 minutes. Remove from the oven and allow to cool completely before peeling off the parchment.

Remove the ice cream from the freezer and allow it to soften for 4–5 minutes before scooping and sandwiching between each pair of biscuits. Gently press together with your hands before serving.

 TIP: These sandwiches can be made in advance and returned to the freezer. Simply remove from the freezer 5 minutes or so before serving.

DARK CHOCOLATE AND FRESH MINT BAKED ALASKA

Zingy and intense, the ice cream for this dessert is flavoured with fresh mint.
A baked Alaska is more doable than you might imagine. In fact, you can make it
in advance and pop the whole thing in the freezer to effortlessly wow your guests
when the time comes to serve. You can freeze the mixture in any small bowl,
as long as it has the same circumference as the cake base.

SERVES 6-8
MAKES AN 18CM (7IN) CAKE

75g (2¾oz) butter, melted,
  plus extra for greasing

60g (2¼oz) dark chocolate
  (minimum 70% cocoa solids),
  finely chopped

2 medium eggs

60g (2¼oz) golden caster sugar

60g (2¼oz) self-raising flour

1 tablespoon good-quality cocoa
  powder, plus extra for dusting

MINT ICE CREAM
MAKES 700ML (1¼ PINTS)

40g (1½oz) mint leaves

200g (9oz) golden caster sugar

125g (4½oz) mascarpone

325g (11½oz) full-fat natural yogurt

50g (2½oz) dark chocolate
  (minimum 70% cocoa solids), cut
  into bite-sized chunks

MERINGUE

180g (6¼oz) caster sugar

3 large egg whites, at room
  temperature

Start with the ice cream. Pick the mint leaves from their stems and put them into a food processor with the sugar. Blitz until combined to a smooth, bright green sugar and then blend with the mascarpone and the yogurt. Stir through the dark chocolate. Line a small 700ml (1¼ pints) pudding basin (13.5cm/5¼in diameter) with clingfilm and pour in the ice-cream mixture. Cover and put in the freezer for at least 4 hours, or preferably overnight, until firm.

To prepare the cake, preheat the oven to 180°C/fan 160°C/gas mark 4, line an 18cm (7in) round cake tin with baking parchment, and lightly grease a baking tray. Melt the butter and chocolate in a bowl set over a saucepan of simmering water or in the microwave. Set aside.

Using an electric whisk or handheld beaters, beat the eggs and sugar together until light and fluffy, about 3–4 minutes. Pour in the melted butter and chocolate and continue to beat until fully combined. Sift in the flour and cocoa and stir until the mixture is smooth and uniform. Spoon the mixture into the prepared tin and bake for 16–18 minutes, until the sponge is well-risen and a skewer inserted into the centre comes out clean. Set the cake aside to cool.

Once the cake is cool and the ice cream frozen, you're ready to assemble the baked alaska. Remove the ice cream from the pudding basin by pulling the clingfilm. Place on a plate or board and ensure there is no remaining clingfilm. Set the ice cream on top of the cake and use as a guide to cut a round of cake exactly the diameter of the base of the ice cream. (Disclaimer: there will be some leftover cake. Donate to a willing recipient.) Keep the cake circle underneath the ice cream and return to the freezer while you make the meringue.

Put the sugar and egg whites in a large, clean metal bowl and set over a pan of simmering water, ensuring that the base of the bowl is not in contact with the water. Cook for 5–7 minutes, scraping down the sides of the bowl and stirring occasionally with a rubber spatula until the sugar has melted and the liquid is warm, smooth and slightly cloudy. Pour this liquid into the bowl of a stand mixer or alternatively, use an electric whisk. Whisk on high for 10–12 minutes until the meringue is cool to the touch and forms stiff peaks.

Transfer the cake and ice cream onto the greased baking tray. Spoon the meringue over the top and sides to cover completely, and use a fork to create peaks. Return to the freezer for an hour.

Preheat the oven to 220°C/fan 200°C/gas mark 7. When ready to serve, cook the baked alaska for 8–10 minutes, until lightly browned. Dust with cocoa powder and serve immediately, in slices.

 TIP: If you don't have quite the correct-sized pudding basin, most bowls will work, just make sure they are freezer proof. Aim for one of roughly 700ml (1¼ pints) capacity with sides as deep as you can find.

FLUFFY BUTTERMILK PANCAKES WITH ROASTED APPLE, TOASTED OATS AND ICE CREAM

These pancakes are epic at breakfast and they make a brilliantly indulgent pudding, too. The combination of caramelized apples and fragrant toasted oats is truly autumnal – just perfect for celebrating the changing season. The addition of whisked egg white gives the pancakes their distinctive fluffiness, so don't skip that step. Serve after leaf-kicking or conker-hunting and compete to see who can pile 'em the highest.

....

SERVES 4 GENEROUSLY
MAKES 12 PANCAKES

ROASTED APPLES

4 eating apples, preferably Russet

4 tablespoons clear honey

3 tablespoons balsamic vinegar

1 teaspoon cinnamon

PANCAKES

150g (5½oz) self-raising flour

½ teaspoon bicarbonate of soda

1 tablespoon golden caster sugar

A pinch of fine salt

2 medium eggs, separated

2 teaspoons vanilla extract

300ml (9½fl oz) buttermilk

Oil, for greasing

25g (1oz) butter, for frying the oats

40g (1½oz) jumbo oats

TO SERVE

4 scoops Vanilla Ice Cream

Maple syrup

Preheat the oven to 200°C/fan 180°C/gas mark 6.

Halve each apple and remove the core using a sharp knife. Put the apple halves, cut side up, into a medium baking dish, in a single layer. Mix the honey, balsamic vinegar and cinnamon to a thick paste and drizzle over the halved apples. Cover and bake for 40 minutes, turning the apples over after 20 minutes, until they are very soft.

Meanwhile, make the pancakes. Put the flour, bicarbonate of soda, sugar and salt in a large bowl, stir well and set aside.

In another bowl, mix the egg yolks, vanilla and buttermilk and combine thoroughly.

Put the egg whites in a third large, clean bowl and whisk using an electric mixer until they form soft peaks.

Make a well in the centre of the dry mix and add the egg and buttermilk mixture. Whisk lightly then, using a light touch, fold through the egg whites in two additions. Once the mixture is uniform, set aside for 5 minutes.

Place a large, non-stick frying pan over a medium heat to get hot, then lightly grease with oil. Working in batches, dollop generous tablespoonfuls of the batter into the pan, spaced well apart, to make pancakes roughly 12cm (4½in) diameter and 1cm (½in) thick. Cook for 1–1½ minutes on each side, or until bubbles form on the surface. Remove to a plate and keep warm. Repeat to make 12.

To toast the oats, heat a small frying pan over a medium heat and add the butter. When it melts and foams, add the oats and cook for 3–4 minutes, stirring continuously, until they are toasted. Remove from the heat.

To serve, for each portion layer up three pancakes with two apple halves and a scoop of ice cream. Drizzle with any warm sauce from the roasted apples and a little maple syrup and then scatter over some toasted oats. If you're after a more dramatic look, squish down a ball of ice cream to a rough disc shape and put atop a pancake. Continue building a tower in this way, using a skewer down the centre of the pile for structure. Top with some roasted apples, any warm sauce from the roasted apples and a little maple syrup and then scatter over the toasted oats. Serve any remaining roasted apples alongside.

 TIPS: Do leave the batter mixture to sit for 5 minutes, as it gives the flour a chance to absorb the liquid and provides the pancake with more structure. And while we're talking about tips, use a piece of kitchen paper to wipe clean the frying pan after cooking each batch; this creates an even, fine greaseproof surface to cook on.

VANILLA ARCTIC ROLL WITH APRICOT CRÈME FRAÎCHE ICE CREAM

A nostalgic nod to the beloved retro artic roll. Imagine a traditional Swiss roll, slathered with apricot jam and filled with crème fraîche ice cream. Or don't imagine it – make it for yourself and tuck right in. Sprinkle your masterpiece with icing sugar and serve it in generous slices. Everyone will be coming back for seconds, just like old times.

SERVES 8

SWISS ROLL

3 large eggs

85g (3oz) golden caster sugar,
 plus extra for dusting

Zest of 1 unwaxed lemon

1 tablespoon warm water

85g (3oz) plain flour

Icing sugar, for dusting

FILLING

½ quantity Crème Fraîche
 Ice Cream (page 21)

6 tablespoons apricot jam

First, prepare the filling. Place a piece of baking parchment on the work surface and scoop the ice cream into the centre to form a log roughly 30cm (12in) long, just shorter than a Swiss roll tin. Use the parchment to roll up the ice cream into a log, twist the ends and return to the freezer to refreeze.

Preheat the oven to 190°C/fan 170°C/gas mark 5. Line a 33cm x 23cm (13 x 9in) Swiss roll tin with baking parchment.

For the Swiss roll, using an electric whisk, beat the eggs and sugar together for 4–5 minutes, until the mixture is very pale in colour and the whisk leaves a trail on the surface of the mixture. Fold in the lemon zest and the warm water, then sift in the flour, a third at a time, folding it gently into the egg mixture using a large spoon.

Pour the mixture into the prepared tin, spread it evenly and bake in the oven for 10–12 minutes, or until the centre springs back when touched.

Meanwhile, place a second sheet of baking parchment on the work surface and dust it liberally with caster sugar. Take the sponge out of the oven and invert it onto the sugared paper. Remove the tin and carefully peel away the baking parchment. Score 1cm (½in) from the edge all the way along one of the long edges, so the sponge tucks inwards easily. Roll up the sponge with the sugared parchment inside and leave to cool on a wire rack.

Once cold, unroll and spread with the apricot jam. Unwrap the ice cream log and place, lengthways, in the centre of the sponge. Wrap the sponge around it and return to the freezer, wrapped in baking parchment or clingfilm, until ready to serve.

Remove the artic roll from the freezer, unwrap and allow it to sit for 5 minutes or so before dusting with icing sugar and cutting into slices to serve.

 TIP: This recipe is equally lovely made with fig jam and the Honey, Fig and Thyme Ice Cream on page 16.

GIANT SOFT FRYING PAN COOKIE

Pure joy and gooey, melty deliciousness. We love this recipe because it's the perfect sharing dish to rustle up for a group of friends – a truly sociable finale to a home-cooked meal. Pile ice cream in the middle of the still-warm cookie, then pop the pan in the centre of the table and let everyone dig in. Expect swooning, lip smacking, giggling, a bit of mess and second helpings all round. When we first created this recipe, our dad, Theo, was spotted polishing off every last crumb...

SERVES 8
MAKES A 28CM (11IN) COOKIE

200g (7oz) unsalted butter, softened

200g (7oz) soft light brown sugar

100g (3½oz) golden caster sugar

1 large egg

1 teaspoon vanilla extract

325g (11½oz) plain flour

½ teaspoon bicarbonate of soda

1 teaspoon baking powder

½ teaspoon sea salt

200g (7oz) chocolate, a mixture of white, dark and milk, chopped into bite-sized chunks

100g (3½oz) hazelnuts, very roughly chopped

Ice cream of choice, to serve

Beat the butter and sugars together in a large bowl for 2 minutes, until light and fluffy. Beat in the egg and vanilla extract. Sift the flour, bicarbonate of soda and baking powder together; scrunch the salt over. Stir into the egg mixture to form a dough. Mix through the chocolate and hazelnuts, cover and chill in the refrigerator for an hour to firm up.

Preheat the oven to 180°C/fan 160°C/gas mark 4.

Spoon the cookie dough into a 28cm (11in) ovenproof frying pan and roughly flatten using the back of a spoon. Bake for 20 minutes until pale golden. Remove from the oven and leave to cool for a few minutes (remember the frying pan handle will be very hot) before placing the pan in the middle of the table with scoops of ice cream placed in the centre of the cookie. All dive in.

FROZEN ETON MESS

Everyone loves the informality of a good Eton Mess. This is a pile-it-all-in kind of pud, and all the better for it. It's also a true cheat's ice cream, ready in an instant. You can even make it to order, when your guests are sitting at the ready, spoons in hand. Pop it in the middle of the table and let everyone help themselves. Try making a tropical version for a fun twist on the classic berry version. Think frozen mango in the ice cream, combined with meringue, kiwi fruit and papaya to serve.

SERVES 8

CHEAT'S BERRY ICE CREAM

250g (9oz) frozen summer berries

250ml (9fl oz) good-quality, ready-made cold custard

2 tablespoons cassis (optional)

TO SERVE

300g (10½oz) strawberries, hulled and quartered

3 large meringues (page 163), crushed into bite-sized pieces, or 150g (5½oz) mini meringues

Mint or basil leaves, roughly chopped, to decorate

Get all the components of this pudding ready beforehand, because once the berry ice cream is made it's a serve-immediately kind of dish.

Empty the frozen berries into the bowl of a food processor and add the custard and cassis, if using. Blend until you have an instant, soft-scoop ice cream.

Pile the ice cream into a large mixing bowl with three-quarters of the strawberries and three-quarters of the meringue. Mix sparingly and quickly until roughly combined; you're not looking for a smooth purée.

Pile into a serving dish, top with the remaining strawberries and meringue and decorate with the herb leaves.

STACKED ICE CREAM CHEESECAKE

There are few greater pleasures than slicing into the layers of this beauty and serving up the colours of autumn in their full glory. And this recipe isn't tricky, merely inventive. It's actually one cracking ice-cream recipe, divided into two, with each batch given its own unique addition. This flavour combination continues to blow our mind: rich maple syrup, warm cinnamon, juicy blackberries, dark chocolate and succulent pink figs were made to be together. Ice cream isn't just for summer!

....

SERVES 8 GENEROUSLY
MAKES A LARGE 900G (2LB)
LOAF CAKE

CINNAMON AND MAPLE ICE CREAM

1 x 397g (14oz) can condensed milk

2 tablespoons maple syrup

1 teaspoon vanilla bean paste
  or extract

450ml (16fl oz) double cream

1 teaspoon ground cinnamon

CHEESECAKE BASE

40g (1½oz) pecan nuts, toasted

150g (5½oz) ginger biscuits

50g (1¾oz) unsalted butter, melted

BLACKBERRY ICE CREAM

80g (2¾oz) juicy blackberries

1 tablespoon dark muscovado sugar

TO SERVE

40g (1½oz) dark chocolate (minimum
  70% cocoa solids)

6–8 ripe pink figs, trimmed
  and quartered

Line the bottom and sides of a 900g (2lb) loaf tin with baking parchment. For the cheesecake base, blitz the toasted nuts and ginger biscuits in a food processor to a fine crumb. Add the melted butter and continue to pulse until the mixture comes together. Spoon the crumbs into the lined tin and press firmly into an even layer. Place in the refrigerator for 40 minutes to firm up.

For the ice creams, mix together the condensed milk, maple syrup and vanilla in a large bowl until combined. In a separate bowl, lightly whip the cream to a soft dropping consistency. Gently fold the cream into the condensed milk mixture until smooth. Divide this mixture between two bowls and stir the cinnamon into one half. Pour the cinnamon ice-cream mixture over the biscuit base and freeze for 4–5 hours or overnight, until firm.

Meanwhile, gently mash the blackberries and brown sugar together to produce a heavy, dark mixture. Stir this through the reserved ice-cream base and combine until well mixed. Cover with clingfilm and place in the refrigerator until ready to pour over the cinnamon layer. It will happily sit overnight.

Once the cinnamon layer has frozen hard, spoon over the blackberry layer and return to the freezer for 4–5 hours.

When ready to serve, melt the chocolate in a bowl set over a saucepan of simmering water or in the microwave. Remove the pudding from the freezer and turn out of the tin (a round-bladed or palette knife will help) then place on a board. Spoon over the melted chocolate and set the figs on the chocolate, pushing slightly so they stay put. Allow the ice cream to soften slightly, then serve in slices.

RED VELVET
ICE CREAM SANDWICHES

The stuff dessert dreams are made of. Delicious sweet domed ice cream sandwiches. If you've got the time (and patience), try making mini versions. They're so cute, your baking will go viral online in minutes. Scarlet, sweet and rather special, these could be a heart-winning gift on Valentine's Day.

MAKES 8

75g (2³/₄oz) unsalted butter, softened

125g (4¹/₂oz) soft light brown sugar

1 medium egg

1 teaspoon vanilla extract

¹/₂ teaspoon baking powder

175g (6oz) plain flour

50ml (2fl oz) buttermilk

1 tablespoon good-quality red food colouring

A pinch of salt

TO SERVE

8 scoops Vanilla Ice Cream (page 14)

Icing sugar, for dusting

Preheat the oven to 180°C/fan 160°C/gas mark 4 and line three baking trays with baking parchment.

Put the butter and sugar in the bowl of a food processor and beat for 3 minutes until light and fluffy. Add the egg and vanilla extract and beat until well combined. Add the baking powder. With the machine on low speed, beat in the flour and buttermilk alternately. Finally, beat in the food colouring and salt.

Spoon the batter into a piping bag fitted with a 1cm (½in) plain nozzle. Pipe the batter onto the lined baking trays to form 16 large circles, roughly 7cm (2¾ in) diameter. Leave a 4cm (1½in) space between them as they will spread on cooking.

Bake for 16–18 minutes, or until they are puffed up and spring back to the touch. Cool on the baking trays.

Remove the ice cream from the freezer and allow it to soften for 4–5 minutes before scooping and sandwiching it between each pair of biscuits. Gently press together with your hands before serving, dusted with icing sugar.

 TIP: These sandwiches can be made in advance and returned to the freezer. Simply remove from the freezer 5 minutes or so before serving.

CINNAMON PAVLOVA
WITH **WINTER FRUIT**

We're pleased to give winter fruit more culinary airtime and to give trusty clementines a new lease of life right here! This glorious dessert is made using the same technique as Granny Dorsey's famous meringues (page 163).

SERVES 8
MAKES A 25CM (10IN) PAVLOVA

PAVLOVA

300g (10½oz) caster sugar

5 large egg whites, at room temperature

1 tablespoon ground cinnamon

TO SERVE

8–10 scoops of Vanilla Ice Cream (page 14), softened

3 clementines, peeled and each segment sliced in half lengthways

Seeds of 1 large pomegranate

Mint leaves

Pistachio nibs, roughly chopped

Preheat the oven to 150°C/fan 130°C/gas mark 2 and line a large baking tray with baking parchment. Draw a large circle with a 25cm (10in) diameter, on the underside of the parchment (ensuring no ink will be in contact with the meringue).

For the pavlova, put the sugar and egg whites in a large metal bowl and set over a pan of simmering water, ensuring that the base of the bowl is not in contact with the water. Cook for 5–7 minutes, scraping down the sides of the bowl and stirring occasionally with a rubber spatula until the sugar has melted and the liquid is warm, smooth and slightly cloudy. Pour this liquid into the bowl of a stand mixer or use an electric handheld whisk.

Whisk on high for 10–12 minutes until the meringue is cool to the touch and forms stiff peaks. Sprinkle the cinnamon over the meringue and fold through, but don't overmix; it's nice to see swirls of cinnamon through the meringue.

Spoon the meringue onto the parchment in a large circle, using the template as a guide. Form a crater by making the sides a little higher than the centre – remember it will increase in size as the pavlova dries out. Transfer the tray to the middle of the oven and immediately reduce the temperature to 120°C/fan 100°C/gas mark ½. Cook the pavlova for 2–2½ hours, until the outside is crispy and the inside is marshmallow-like.

Remove the tray from the oven and allow the pavlova to cool completely on the tray. Carefully peel off the baking parchment and transfer the pavlova to a flat board or plate.

Pile the ice cream balls into the centre of the pavlova and top with the clementine segments and pomegranate seeds. Serve straight away, decorated with mint and pistachio nibs.

CHAPTER 3

BAKES & PUDDINGS

We grew up on classic British puddings so, of
course, we couldn't let this book come together
without devoting a chapter to some of our childhood
favourites. When we were little, family celebrations
were always topped off with some kind of much-loved
bake, like a Sticky Toffee Pudding (page 118). We're
thrilled they've made their way onto these pages.
Other more modern favourites include the Collapsed
Espresso Cake (page 112) and our Elderflower
Celebration Cake (page 122). We hope you enjoy
making these treats for friends and family, or even just
for fun. Oh, and do give the Cinnamon Buns (page
102) a go as soon as you get a chance. They
always dazzle and delight in equal measure.

CINNAMON BUNS

This recipe is one of our absolute favourites. In recent years, we've made a few trips to Stockholm and Copenhagen where these buns are found in every bakery. Each time, we wanted to bring back suitcases of these sweet 'n' spicy delights. By creating this recipe, we no longer need to. At heart, this is a simple bun. But it's spectacular.

MAKES 12 LARGE BUNS

6 cardamom pods

300ml (½ pint) whole milk

50g (1¾oz) unsalted butter

450g (1lb) strong white flour,
  plus extra for dusting

2 teaspoons ground cinnamon

7g (¼ oz) fast-action dried yeast

50g (1¾oz) caster sugar

½ teaspoon salt

2 medium free-range eggs

1 tablespoon olive oil, for oiling

FILLING

100g (3½oz) salted butter, softened

80g (2¾oz) soft dark brown sugar

2 teaspoons ground cinnamon

1 teaspoon ground nutmeg

½ teaspoon salt

GLAZE

150g (5½oz) icing sugar

Juice of ½ lemon

1–2 tablespoons water

TO DECORATE

30g (1oz) sugar nibs or
  pearl sugar (optional)

Bruise the cardamom pods hard enough to split them and shake their black seeds into a mortar. Crush to a rough powder with a pestle and put into a saucepan along with the milk. Warm over a gentle heat for 5 minutes or so, removing from the heat just as the milk begins to simmer. Stir the butter into the pan to melt in the residual heat. Cool for 10 minutes or so.

Meanwhile, sift the flour into a large mixing bowl with the cinnamon, dried yeast, sugar and salt and mix until combined. Make a well in the centre and add the eggs and warm milk and mix until everything comes together to make a very soft, sticky dough. Knead for 10 minutes using an electric dough hook or alternatively, turn the sticky dough onto an oiled surface and knead until smooth, about 10-12 minutes. The dough should be smooth and spring back a little when pressed. Put the dough in an oiled bowl, cover it with an oiled piece of clingfilm and leave to rise at room temperature for 45–60 minutes, until doubled in size.

Meanwhile, make the filling. Beat all the ingredients together with a wooden spoon until you have a thick paste. Set aside.

Once the dough has risen, divide it in half, place each one on a lightly floured or oiled surface and roll each one out to a large, long 30 x 46cm (12 x 18in) rectangle. Spread the paste over the rectangles, keeping a clear 2cm (1in) border around the edges. Roll each piece of dough into a fat cylinder and then, using a sharp knife, cut into six 6cm (2½in) slices. Nestle the slices into a large 25 x 35cm (10 x 14in) ceramic baking dish or roasting tin. Cover once again and leave for a final prove of 45–50 minutes.

Preheat the oven to 200°C/fan 180°C/gas mark 6. Bake the buns in the oven for 16–18 minutes until slightly puffed and golden brown.

Make the glaze by mixing all the ingredients to a smooth paste.

Remove the buns from the oven and allow them to cool in the dish. Drizzle the glaze over and sprinkle with sugar nibs, if using.

GINGERBREAD COWBARN

A gingerbread house – or indeed, a barn – is a labour of love, so don't embark on this one unless you really have the time to do it justice. We've based this on our family's Hampshire dairy barn where Jude's first began, and we now make one every Christmas with the little ones. Along the way, we've learned new traditions are just as important as old ones.

SERVES 15
MAKES 1 LARGE BARN

300g (10½oz) golden syrup
 or clear honey

400g (14oz) soft light brown sugar

400g (14oz) unsalted butter

Zest of 2 unwaxed lemons

2 teaspoons bicarbonate of soda

1kg (2lb 4oz) plain flour

2 tablespoons ground ginger

4 teaspoons ground cinnamon

1 teaspoon ground nutmeg

½ teaspoon ground cloves

2 teaspoons salt

2 medium eggs, lightly beaten

ROYAL ICING

250g (9oz) icing sugar

1 medium egg white, lightly beaten

½ teaspoon lemon juice

YOU WILL NEED

Firm paper or card to cut out
 templates on pages 170–171

2 x wooden poles/twigs, roughly
 12cm (4½in) and marzipan to
 secure the poles

Toy animals and trees, to decorate

Put the golden syrup, sugar, butter and lemon zest into a very large saucepan and place over a medium heat. Heat, stirring frequently, until the sugar has dissolved. Increase the heat slightly until the mixture reaches boiling point and then, working quickly, remove the saucepan from the heat and beat in the bicarbonate of soda briefly until combined. Set the saucepan aside to cool for 15 minutes.

Sift the flour, spices and salt together, then fold them into the melted mixture in batches, using a wooden spoon. Mix in the eggs until just combined, but be cautious not to overwork the mixture or the biscuits will spread during baking.

The dough will be very sticky to begin with, but resist adding more flour. Scrape the sticky dough out of the saucepan onto a clean, oiled surface and knead together until just smooth. Wrap in clingfilm and chill in the refrigerator for an hour.

Make your versions of the templates using firm paper or card. Cut a large sheet of greaseproof paper and roll out the gingerbread on it to a thickness of 8mm (⅜in). Using the templates as a guide, cut out house pieces from the gingerbread, but leave on the paper for ease. Transfer the gingerbread pieces, still on the paper, to a couple of baking trays and put in the freezer for 10 minutes to firm up completely.

Preheat the oven to 160°C/fan 140°C/gas mark 3. Bake the gingerbread in batches for 12–15 minutes until golden brown at the edges. Leave to cool on the baking trays for 10 minutes, before transferring to a wire rack to cool completely.

Meanwhile, make the icing. Sift the icing sugar into the bowl of an electric mixer. Add the beaten egg white and lemon juice. Whisk, on low speed (to avoid incorporating too much air into the icing), for 2–3 minutes, until the consistency is smooth, stiff but not too wet. If the icing seems too dry and crumbly, add a little water. If it looks slightly runny, add a little extra icing sugar. Transfer to a piping bag fitted with a small plain nozzle, ready for piping.

To assemble the gingerbread barn, pipe icing down both sides of a gable end. Attach a side wall at right angles and hold together for a few moments while the icing hardens, then use cans or jars to support the walls while they set. Continue to stick the gingerbread together by attaching another wall and the back gable so you have the walls for the barn. Leave to set for 1 hour before you add the roof.

Decorate the side walls of the house by piping royal icing to make windows and the front door surround before you add the roof (the overhang can make this tricky).

Lay the roof pieces flat and, with a steady hand, pipe on roof tiles. Secure the wooden poles each in a ball of marzipan to take the weight of the large, overhanging roof. Pipe the remaining icing along the tops of the four walls and gently lower the roof pieces into place.

Leave the barn to set for a further 2 hours. Decorate with toy barn animals and trees. Serve.

ICE CREAM CUPCAKES

Cupcakes are now a firm favourite at parties, bake sales and tea time. Here's a fun way to present them, with a Jude's twist. Make sure the icing is really soft – you want it to look just like ice cream! These are decorated with a flake, as every classic soft serve should be.

MAKES 12 CUPCAKES

CUPCAKES

200g (7oz) unsalted butter, softened

200g (7oz) golden caster sugar

3 medium eggs, lightly beaten

100g (3½oz) ground almonds

120g (4¼oz) self-raising flour, sifted

LEMON BUTTERCREAM

240g (8¾oz) unsalted butter,
 softened

500g (1lb 2 oz) icing sugar, sifted

2 teaspoons vanilla extract

Zest of 2 unwaxed lemons

Up to 2 tablespoons whole milk

TO SERVE

6 chocolate flakes, halved

Preheat the oven to 180°C/fan 160°C/gas mark 4 and line a 12-hole cupcake tray with paper cases.

For the cupcakes, using an electric mixer, beat together the butter and sugar for 5 minutes until light and fluffy. Beat in the eggs, a little at a time, until well combined. Fold through the ground almonds and flour. Spoon the mixture into the paper cases, filling them no more than three-quarters full.

Bake for 15–18 minutes, or until a skewer inserted into the centre comes out clean and the tops are lightly browned. Transfer to a wire rack and allow the cupcakes to cool completely before icing.

To make the buttercream, beat the butter in a bowl until light and fluffy. Slowly mix in the icing sugar. Once combined, and with the mixer on low, add the vanilla, lemon zest and just enough milk to make the mixture creamy and of a soft piping consistency. Increase the speed to high and continue to beat for a further 2–3 minutes until the buttercream is very light and fluffy.

Spoon into a piping bag fitted with 1cm (½in) star nozzle and pipe the buttercream onto the cooled cupcakes. Insert a chocolate flake half into the buttercream on each one, and serve.

JULIA'S DOUBLE CHOCOLATE BROWNIES

Gooey. Indulgent. Dense. The stuff of dreams. This brownie is the most 'brownie' brownie you'll ever try. The recipe was inspired by our dear friend Julia, who's known far and wide for her remarkable brownies. She even makes brownie mountain wedding cakes! Good news – these squares freeze beautifully, so don't be afraid to double-up on the ingredients and make a bumper batch.

MAKES 16–20

250g (9oz) dark chocolate (minimum 70% cocoa solids), broken into 2–3cm (¾–1¼in) pieces

200g (7oz) butter, cut into 2–3cm (¾–1¼in) cubes

440g (15½oz) golden caster sugar

4 medium eggs

50g (1¾oz) self-raising flour

50g (1¾oz) cocoa powder

TO DECORATE

50g (1¾oz) dark chocolate (minimum 70% cocoa solids), melted

40g (1½oz) freeze-dried strawberries – a mixture of larger and smaller pieces (optional)

Preheat the oven to 180°C/fan 160°C/gas mark 4 and line a 23cm (9in) square tin with baking parchment.

Put the chocolate and butter into a large saucepan and melt over a very gentle heat, stirring regularly to ensure the bottom does not burn. Once completely melted, remove from the heat, transfer to a bowl and stir through the caster sugar.

Crack one egg into the mixture at a time and, using a wooden spoon, beat in each egg thoroughly before adding the next. When all are fully incorporated, sift over the flour and cocoa powder. Continue to mix until everything is evenly distributed. Spoon or pour the batter into the prepared tin and bake for 30 minutes until the brownie has cooked but is still a little gooey in the centre – it will continue to cook on cooling. Remove from the oven and leave to cool completely in the tin.

Remove the brownie from the tin and set on a wire rack. To decorate, spread over the melted chocolate using a palette knife. Sprinkle over the freeze-dried strawberries and allow the chocolate to set. Cut into squares to serve.

 TIP: We're so in love with these, we've turned them into an ice cream by folding pieces of brownie into a chocolatey scoop – have a go!

COLLAPSED ESPRESSO CHOCOLATE CAKE

Coffee desserts are the perfect after-dinner perk-me-up. And there's something about the combination of dark chocolate and intense espresso that is just so right. The key here is to make a strong meringue, and be extra gentle when it comes to mixing. Serve this warm, in soft, gooey slices.

SERVES 8
MAKES A 23CM (9IN) CAKE

Cold butter, for greasing

75g (2¾oz) whole blanched almonds

250g (9oz) dark chocolate (minimum 70% cocoa solids), roughly chopped

150g (5½oz) salted butter

250g (9oz) golden caster sugar

100g (3½oz) icing sugar, plus extra for dusting

6 medium eggs, separated

30ml (1fl oz) espresso shot

A pinch of salt

TO SERVE

Cocoa powder, sifted

Ice cream of choice

Preheat the oven to 170°C/fan 150°C/gas mark 3 and lightly butter and line a 23cm (9in) springform cake tin with baking parchment.

Tip the almonds onto a baking tray and toast in the oven for 8 minutes. Blitz in a food processor to a fine powder dust. Set aside.

Melt the chocolate and butter in a heatproof bowl set over a saucepan of simmering water or in the microwave. Remove from the heat and mix in 60g (2¼oz) of the golden caster sugar. Then add the egg yolks, almonds and espresso.

Put the egg whites into a large, clean bowl with the salt and whisk using an electric whisk until they hold soft peaks. Whisk in half the remaining golden caster sugar until the mixture will stand up in peaks when the whisk is lifted, then add the rest of the golden caster and icing sugar. Whisk again until you have a stiff and glossy meringue. Stir a spoonful into the chocolate mixture to loosen it slightly, then gently fold in the rest (be careful not to knock out all of the air). Pour the batter into the prepared tin, level the top and bake for 25–30 minutes.

Leave the cake to cool in the tin for 15 minutes. Don't worry – it will sink dramatically and the surface will crack, but this all adds to the charm. Once cool, remove from the tin and dust with icing sugar and cocoa powder and serve warm, alongside ice cream.

MAPLE PUMPKIN PIE
WITH STREUSEL PECANS

We've taken a classic Thanksgiving foodie favourite and added some extra flair. The streusel element of this recipe is truly delicious and brings plenty of crunch to the mix, contrasting the smoothness of the pumpkin. This pie is perfect for topping off a long, lazy lunch on a cold, crisp autumn afternoon. Save us a slice!

SERVES 10
MAKES A 20CM (8IN) PIE

CRUST

225g (8oz) ginger nut biscuits or ginger snaps

75g (2¾oz) butter

PIE FILLING

500g (1lb 2oz) pumpkin flesh, peeled, deseeded and cubed

¼ teaspoon ground nutmeg

¼ teaspoon ground ginger

¼ teaspoon ground cinnamon

4 tablespoons maple syrup

4 tablespoons single cream

5 medium egg yolks

STREUSEL

50g (1¾oz) unsalted butter, softened

50g (1¾oz) plain flour

50g (1¾oz) light brown soft sugar

75g (2¾oz) pecans, roughly chopped

½ teaspoon ground cinnamon

TO SERVE

Ice cream of choice

Preheat the oven to 180°C/fan 160°C/gas mark 4 and base-line a 20cm (8in) loose-based flan tin with baking parchment.

Begin by making the crust. Tip the ginger biscuits into a food processor and process to a crumb before transferring to a medium bowl. Melt the butter in a small saucepan – don't be afraid to keep cooking until the butter browns slightly, this only adds to the overall taste. Pour the butter over the crumbs and mix well.

Press the buttery biscuit mix into the lined tin and, using a spatula, push the mixture about 2cm (¾in) up the sides to form a rim. Chill the crust in the refrigerator for 20 minutes to harden up.

Place the tin on a baking sheet (this makes for a more even bake) and transfer to the oven for 8–10 minutes. Remove and allow to cool slightly.

Meanwhile, for the filling, bring a small pan of water to the boil and add the pumpkin. Simmer for about 15 minutes until the flesh is tender and cuts like butter. Drain well, allowing the pumpkin to steam dry for a few minutes before puréeing until smooth. Mix the purée with the spices, maple syrup, cream and egg yolks. Pour into the crust and bake for 20–25 minutes until just set with a slight wobble. Remember, the filling will have a second bake once topped with the streusel.

Meanwhile, make the streusel. Put the butter, flour and sugar in a mixing bowl and rub together using your hands until the mix has come together. Stir through the pecans and cinnamon.

Remove the pie from the oven and top with the streusel mix. Return to the oven to cook the pie for a further 15 minutes. Allow the pie to cool slightly before serving in slices with a scoop of ice cream.

APRICOT AND FRANGIPANE TART

The fine art of frangipane is well worth mastering. Once you've grasped the basics, you can get creative. Here, it's all about stirring the almonds through the cake batter to make a delicious, dense, subtly nutty tart. The apricots could easily be switched out for apples, if you prefer a more traditional touch. Oh, and glazing with apricot jam is worth the extra step to showcase your pastry chef skills!

SERVES 10–12
MAKES A 26CM (10½IN) TART

PASTRY

225g (8oz) plain flour, plus
  extra for dusting

140g (5oz) cold butter

1 medium egg

A pinch of salt

60g (2¼oz) golden caster sugar

FRANGIPANE FILLING

175g (6oz) butter, at room
  temperature

175g (6oz) golden caster sugar

175g (6oz) ground almonds

2 large eggs

A few drops of almond extract

TOPPING

450g (1lb) apricots (about 10),
  halved and stoned

100g (3½oz) smooth apricot jam

Juice of ½ lemon

Preheat the oven to 200°C/fan 180°C/gas mark 6 and put a baking sheet on the middle shelf to heat. Lightly butter a 26cm (10½in) loose-based flan tin and dust with flour.

To make the pastry, put all the ingredients in a food processor and whizz everything together until the mix forms a ball. Roll it out on a lightly floured surface into a thin round, large enough to line the flan tin. Lift the pastry by rolling it round a rolling pin and then unrolling it over the tin. Don't worry if the pastry cracks; it is so rich you can just press with your fingers to seal the cracks. Ease the pastry into the bottom corners and use the rolling pin to roll firmly right across the top to trim away any excess pastry.

To make the filling, whizz everything together in the food processor (no need to wash the bowl after the pastry), and spread evenly in the pastry case. Lay the apricots, cut side down, on the frangipane in a circular pattern, starting at the rim. Gently press them into the frangipane.

Place the tart on the hot baking sheet on the middle shelf of the oven. Bake for 30 minutes, then turn down the heat to 180°C/fan 160°C/gas mark 4 and bake for a further 15–20 minutes or until the filling is set and brown. Remove from the oven.

Melt the jam with the lemon juice in a small, heavy-based pan over a low heat. Brush or spoon it carefully all over the apricots and frangipane.

When still just warm, turn the tart out of the flan tin. Serve warm with cream or ice cream for a pudding, or cold in thin slices as a teatime treat.

STICKY
TOFFEE PUDDING

Few things can top this pudding. It's all about the detail. We love to spread half the toffee sauce on the base of the pudding dish before spooning the sponge cake mixture on top. It makes for a wonderfully squidgy bottom. Whenever we revisit this recipe, it brings back fond childhood memories – sticky toffee puddings were baked in abundance when we were growing up. We couldn't help turning the British treat into a beautiful ice cream, rippled through with pudding pieces. You'll find tubs lining the shelves of Britain's top delis, farm shops and food stores.

SERVES 8

200g (7oz) Medjool dates, stoned and roughly chopped

1 teaspoon bicarbonate of soda

250ml (9fl oz) boiling water

50g (1¾oz) unsalted butter, softened

75g (2¾oz) golden caster sugar

100g (3½oz) dark muscovado sugar

2 medium eggs, beaten

175g (6oz) self-raising flour

A pinch of salt

A pinch of ground cloves

65g (2½oz) stem ginger, finely chopped

SAUCE

115g (4oz) unsalted butter

115g (4oz) soft dark brown sugar

150ml (¼ pint) double cream

TO SERVE

Ice cream of choice

Preheat the oven to 180°C/fan 160°C/gas mark 4.

Begin with the sauce. Simply put all the sauce ingredients into a small saucepan and warm over a medium heat until everything has come together and the sugar has melted. Bring to a gentle simmer and bubble for 3–4 minutes before removing from the heat, stirring all the while. Pour half the sauce into a (2-litre) 3½-pint ceramic ovenproof dish and transfer to the refrigerator. The remaining sauce can happily sit in the saucepan until needed.

To make the pudding, put the dates and bicarbonate of soda into a small saucepan and cover with the boiling water. Bring to the boil and simmer for 5 minutes before removing from the heat and gently mashing with a fork or blitzing to a thick paste with a handheld blender.

Beat the butter and both the sugars together in a bowl until well combined, then add the eggs, one at a time. Beat in the flour, salt and ground cloves and continue to mix until everything is evenly distributed. Stir through the date paste and mix well. Finally, add the stem ginger. Pour the mixture into the ovenproof dish, over the toffee sauce, and transfer to the oven. Bake for 30–35 minutes.

Remove the pudding from the oven before pouring over the remaining toffee sauce, roughly spreading to cover the pudding evenly. Return to the oven for a final 3–4 minutes before placing on the table. Serve with ice cream.

CLEMENTINE, CLOVE AND POLENTA PUDDING CAKE

This gluten-free recipe will become a firm favourite. It's perfect for treating friends and family at home, or for popping in a tin and taking to your host's house. Dream dinner-guest klaxon! The trick is to simmer the oranges until they're super-soft, then pop the whole lot in the food processor, zest, pith and all. This cake is great to make in advance. The flavour is even richer after a couple of days.

SERVES 8
MAKES A 22CM (8½IN) CAKE

400g (14oz) clementines
   (roughly 5 small ones)

Butter, for greasing

6 medium eggs

250g (9oz) golden caster sugar

160g (5¾oz) polenta

80g (2¾oz) ground almonds

1 teaspoon baking powder

½ teaspoon ground cloves

30g (1oz) flaked almonds

Zest of 1 unwaxed orange

CLEMENTINE SYRUP

Juice of 2 clementines

30g (1oz) caster sugar

TO SERVE

Icing sugar, for dusting

Vanilla Ice Cream (page 14)

A handful of pistachio nibs
   (optional)

Wash the clementines and put them in a saucepan. Cover with cold water and bring to the boil. Simmer the oranges for 2 hours. Drain and, when cool, cut each one in half and remove the pips. Put the clementines – skins, pith, flesh and all – in a food processor and give them a quick blitz.

Preheat the oven to 190°C/fan 170°C/gas mark 5. Butter and line a 22cm (8½in) springform cake tin with baking parchment.

Gently beat the eggs by hand in a mixing bowl, adding the sugar, polenta, almonds, baking powder and ground cloves. Mix well before stirring through the pulped clementines.

Pour the cake batter into the prepared tin, scatter with the flaked almonds and orange zest and bake for 50–60 minutes or until the top is golden and a skewer inserted into the centre comes out clean. Remove from the oven and leave to cool, on a wire rack but still in the tin.

Meanwhile, make the syrup by simply warming the clementine juice with the sugar in a small pan over a medium heat. Bring to a simmer and bubble for 1–2 minutes before spooning over the warm cake (whilst the cake is still in the tin).

When the cake is cold, remove it from the tin. Serve, dusted with icing sugar and with dollops of ice cream alongside and a few pistachio nibs scattered over, if desired.

 TIP: Instead of clementines, you can make this with 2 unwaxed oranges or 400g (14oz) kumquats, whichever is your preference.

ELDERFLOWER CELEBRATION CAKE

This one is just the thing for early summer parties. If you're making your own cordial, pick the elderflowers when the sun is shining. It's the perfect excuse for hedgerow scouring and outdoor adventures. We've used raspberries here, but any soft fruit will do. Simply let the season be your guide – use whatever's at its best and most plentiful and you can't go wrong.

SERVES 14–16
MAKES A THREE-TIER 20CM (8IN) CAKE

CAKE

375g (13oz) butter, softened

375g (13oz) golden caster sugar

6 large eggs, lightly beaten

260g (9½oz) self-raising flour, sifted

1 teaspoon baking powder

A pinch of salt

115g (4oz) ground almonds

2 tablespoons elderflower cordial, or extra as needed

BUTTERCREAM

300g (10½oz) unsalted butter, softened

½ teaspoon vanilla extract or vanilla bean paste

450g (1lb) icing sugar

5 tablespoons elderflower cordial

Grated zest of 1 unwaxed lemon

DECORATE

250g (9oz) raspberries

Fresh flowers – elderflowers and peonies, in season

Mini meringues (page 163)

Preheat the oven to 180°C/fan 160°C/gas mark 4 and line 3 x 20cm (8in) round cake tins with baking parchment.

For the cake, using an electric mixer, beat together the butter and sugar for 5 minutes until light and fluffy. Gradually add the eggs, beating well after each addition and adding a tablespoon of flour each time. Fold through the remaining flour, the baking powder, salt, ground almonds and cordial. The mixture should drop easily from a spoon – if it seems a bit stiff, stir in an extra tablespoon or so of cordial. Divide the mixture equally between the prepared tins and spread evenly with a palette knife or the back of a spoon. Bake for about 22–25 minutes until well risen, golden brown and springy. Remove from the oven and cool for 10 minutes in the tins before carefully turning out onto a wire rack to cool completely.

Make the buttercream just before you're ready to assemble the cake so it remains soft and spreadable. Beat the butter and vanilla extract for about 3 minutes until very light. Add the sifted icing sugar and mix (slowly at first to prevent clouds of icing sugar) until very light and fluffy. Mix in the elderflower cordial and lemon zest.

To assemble the cake, remove any baking parchment from the cake bases and place the cakes on a board. If the tops are mounded, use a serrated knife to level them so each layer will sit flush with the next. Spread a generous amount of buttercream over the surface of each of the three cut cake layers, right to the edge. Add raspberries to the surface of the bottom two layers.

Carefully stack the cake layers one on top of the other, enclosing the raspberries. Use a palette knife to smooth the remaining buttercream icing around the edges, removing any excess so that the cake layers are visible. Decorate with fresh flowers and keep in a cool room until serving.

CHAPTER 4

SHAKES, COCKTAILS & SUNDAES

What makes an ice cream dish great? First things first, taste, it must be delicious. This is closely followed by another 'must', fun. We can't think of anything more flavourful and playful than an ice cream sundae or shake. There's just one rule, don't hold back on the sparklers, fan wafers and marshmallows! In this chapter, you'll find an all-star line-up of our favourites, including other-worldly ideas that little ones will love, like our Black and Blue Freakshake (page 126) and the spectacular Knickerbocker Glory (page 144). There are plenty of grown-up treats to be sampled, too, like our Gin, Peach Sorbet and Lime Cocktail (page 135) and the Mini Caramel and Guinness Floats (page 136).

BLACK AND BLUE FREAKSHAKE

This oh-so-out-there deep-hued treat is made with a dark, sticky blueberry purée and tart homemade blackberry ice cream. We suggest picking your own brambles in early autumn, once the summer sunshine has ripened them to their juiciest. Purple fingers and tongues guaranteed! When it comes to assembly, anything goes. Layer your glass with chunks of shortbread if you prefer, or add them as an extra alongside the mini meringues. Get your freak on.

SERVES 4

BLUEBERRY COMPÔTE

175g (6oz) blueberries

1 tablespoon water

1 tablespoon clear honey

TO SERVE

6 scoops Blackberry
  Ice Cream (page 22)

12 mini meringues
  (see tip for Granny Dorsey's
  Gigantic Meringues on page 163)

A handful of blueberries
  and a few blackberries

Silver balls (optional)

For the compôte, put the blueberries, water and honey into a small saucepan and cook over a low heat for 5–6 minutes, stirring intermittently, until the berries burst. If needed, lightly mash with a masher until most berries have been crushed. Remove from the heat and set aside to cool.

To assemble the sundaes, spoon 1–2 tablespoons of compôte into the base of each sundae glass. Build up alternate layers of ice cream, meringues, compôte and blueberries, finishing with a scoop of ice cream, a couple of meringues and some berries. Sprinkle with a few silver balls, if using, and serve immediately.

ULTIMATE VANILLA MILKSHAKE

Here's how to make any milkshake you fancy. We've gone for vanilla and chocolate, but the same rule applies, whatever flavour you're whipping up – two scoops of ice cream to 200ml (7fl oz) of milk. If you're after a classic shake, keep it simple.

SERVES 2

4–5 scoops Vanilla Ice Cream (page 14)

400ml (14fl oz) semi-skimmed milk

Put the ice cream into a blender with the milk and whizz to a thick, pourable consistency. Divide between two glasses and drink straight away.

CHOCOLATE MUDSLIDE SHAKE

If you're up for experimentation, try adding a shot of malt, a handful of marshmallows or any other naughty treats you have to hand.

SERVES 2

4 scoops Dark Chocolate Ice Cream (page 21)

400ml (14fl oz) semi-skimmed milk

4 tablespoons Glossy Hot Chocolate Sauce, at room temperature (page 154)

Put the chocolate ice cream and the milk into a blender and blend until smooth. Drizzle the chocolate sauce around the sides of two milkshake glasses and pour the chocolate shake over the top.

AVOCADO, ALMOND MILK AND OAT SHAKE

Rise and shine! Once you've created this frozen avocado smoothie base, you're good to go in the mornings. Freeze it in an ice-cube tray, then pop your cubes straight into a blender for a speedy meal first thing. It's perfect for portion control, and for cutting prep time so you can get some extra shut-eye. Don't forget the lime juice, we think it makes all the difference.

MAKES 2 SHAKES

SHAKE

7–8 cubes of avocado ice cream
 (see recipe below)

200ml (7fl oz) almond milk

2 tablespoons rolled oats

Mint, to decorate

AVOCADO ICE CUBES
MAKES 200ML (7FL OZ)

A handful of mint

1 x 160ml (5½fl oz) can
 coconut cream

1 tablespoon agave syrup
 (or clear honey if not vegan)

Flesh from 1 large, ripe avocado

Juice of 1 lime

For the ice cubes, pick the mint leaves from the stems and put them, along with the coconut cream, into a food processor. Blitz until combined to a smooth, green paste and then blend with the honey, avocado flesh and lime juice. Spoon into an ice-cube tray. Freeze overnight.

For the shake, simply blitz the ice-cream cubes, almond milk and oats in a blender until smooth. Pour into two glasses and serve immediately, decorated with fresh mint.

PEAR, PROSECCO
AND ROSEMARY LOLLIES

Lollies for the grown-ups! These beauties are refreshing, rather sophisticated treats to enjoy in the heat of the sun. So when the weather forecast looks promising, whip up a batch and pop them in your freezer. Rosemary gives these fancy pops an aromatic edge, but any woody herb would be just as delicious – experiment with sage or thyme to see which hits the spot for you.

MAKES 10 X 100ML (3½FL OZ) LOLLIES

300ml (½ pint) cold water

25g (1oz) granulated sugar

3–4 rosemary sprigs

3 pears (about 185g/6½oz each) – about 500g (1lb 2oz) peeled weight

50ml (2fl oz) freshly squeezed lemon juice

200–250ml (7–9fl oz) prosecco

YOU WILL NEED

10 x 100ml (3½fl oz) lolly moulds and sticks

Put the water, sugar and rosemary in a saucepan and bring to a gentle simmer. Cook for 4–5 minutes before removing from the heat and picking out the rosemary sprigs.

Peel and core the pears. Cut the flesh into 2cm (¾in) cubes and put them into the rosemary syrup. Return the saucepan to a low heat, cover and simmer the pears until tender, about 10–12 minutes. Remove from the heat and allow the pears to sit for a few minutes, cooling slightly.

Tip the pears and syrup into a blender, add the lemon juice and blitz until smooth (or simply blitz everything in the saucepan with a stick blender).

Pour the mixture into a large jug and stir through the prosecco to make up the volume to 1 litre (1¾ pints). It will bubble a little, but be patient and the bubbles will dissipate. Stir to combine. Pour the mixture into the lolly moulds, but don't fill them right to the top as the mixture will expand on freezing. Put in the freezer for an hour or so and just as the lollies begin to set, insert the lolly sticks and freeze overnight until firm.

To serve, remove the lollies from the freezer, dip the moulds briefly in hot water, then gently pull the lollies out of the moulds and serve straight away.

GIN, PEACH SORBET AND LIME COCKTAIL

Why use plain old ice cubes to cool your drink when you could use peach sorbet? This remarkable summer cocktail redefines the classic G&T. It's inspired by our long friendship with the renowned London gin makers at Sipsmith. Together, we launched a Gin & Tonic ice cream in 2016. It's still one of our most loved – and instagrammed – flavours. Here, we ran away with the idea and created a tasty tipple that breaks every rule under the sun!

MAKES 1 COCKTAIL

½ unwaxed lime, halved

¼ ripe peach, cut into 3 wedges

2 scoops Summer Peach Sorbet (page 58)

1 shot (25ml/scant 1fl oz) gin, preferably Sipsmith

Tonic water

Squeeze one wedge of lime into the bottom of a cocktail glass. Add a peach wedge or two and the peach sorbet. Pour over the gin and top with tonic water. Serve garnished with the remaining lime and peach wedges.

To serve, wait for the sorbet to melt before sipping leisurely.

MINI CARAMEL AND GUINNESS FLOATS

The luck of the Irish, in float form! Make sure your Guinness is really cold – that's the trick to helping the ice cream stay in shape. And reach for small glasses when it comes to serving, ice cream and Guinness is a deliciously rich combination. This one is perfect for dinner parties, and if you prep it at the table you'll bring a spot of theatre to the occasion.

SERVES 3

6 tablespoons Salted Caramel Sauce (page 154)

6 large scoops Vanilla Ice Cream (page 14)

440ml (15½fl oz) Guinness

Drizzle 1 tablespoon of caramel sauce into the bottom of each glass, then top each with two scoops of ice cream. Slowly pour the Guinness over the ice cream, waiting for any froth to dissipate. Finish with a final drizzle of caramel, and serve.

KEY LIME PIE SUNDAE

A key lime pie, redefined. Think lime cheesecake ice cream with zingy green jelly and a hit of gingerbread. We'll be honest – you'll make too much gingerbread, so go ahead and make a gingerbread man, woman or octopus with the leftovers.

SERVES 4

MAKES 1 LITRE (1¾ PINTS)

JELLY

1 x 135g (5oz) pack lime jelly

LIME CHEESECAKE ICE CREAM

200g (7oz) cream cheese, softened

1 x 397g (14oz) can condensed milk

100ml (3½fl oz) double cream

Zest and juice of 3 large unwaxed limes

A pinch of salt

GINGERBREAD

75g (2¾oz) golden syrup

100g (3½oz) soft light brown sugar

100g (3½oz) unsalted butter

Zest of ½ unwaxed lemon

½ teaspoon bicarbonate of soda

½ teaspoon salt

2 teaspoons ground ginger

250g (9oz) plain flour

1 large egg yolk

TO SERVE

300ml (½ pint) semi-skimmed milk

50g (1¾oz) crystallized ginger, chopped

1 unwaxed lime, finely sliced

Start with the jelly. Line a 900g (2lb) loaf tin with clingfilm. Make 568ml (1 pint) of jelly following the manufacturer's instructions and pour into the lined tin. Transfer to the refrigerator to set. Once it has set, turn out of the loaf tin and cut into cubes.

For the ice cream, put the cream cheese, condensed milk and cream into a large mixing bowl and, using electric handheld beaters, beat until light and creamy, about 1 minute. Add the lime zest, juice and salt and beat until evenly combined, about 30 seconds. Pour into an airtight freezerproof container and freeze for at least 4 hours but preferably overnight, until firm.

Next, make the gingerbread. Put the golden syrup, sugar, butter and lemon zest in a large saucepan over a medium heat for 4–5 minutes, stirring frequently until the butter melts and the sugar has dissolved. Increase the heat slightly until the mixture reaches boiling point. Working quickly, remove the saucepan from the heat, beat in the bicarbonate of soda and salt until combined and the bubbles start to subside. Set the saucepan aside to cool for 15 minutes. Mix the ginger with the flour and add to the pan in batches, folding until evenly mixed. Beat in the egg yolk until the dough just comes together, being careful not to overmix. Gather the dough together into a ball, wrap in clingfilm and put in the refrigerator to chill for an hour.

Preheat the oven to 160°C/fan 140°C/gas mark 3. Roll out the dough on a sheet of greaseproof paper to form a rectangle 15 x 20cm (6 x 8in). (You won't need all of it, but you can shape any remaining into gingerbread men.) Slide the dough, still on the paper, onto a baking sheet. Bake for 15 minutes until golden brown at the edges. Once cool, cut the gingerbread into tall long shards.

To assemble, drop some cubes of jelly into four milkshake glasses. Scoop half the ice cream into a blender and add the milk. Blend until smooth, then pour into the glasses. Add some more jelly, then ice cream and a shard of gingerbread. Serve with any leftover cubes of jelly, the crystallized ginger and slices of lime.

DOUBLE CHOCOLATE SUNDAE

To share, or not to share, that is the question. This sundae screams pure indulgence. We've put together some suggestions to get you started, but this one's all about colouring outside the lines and creating your own glorious, decadent, chocolatey masterpieces. The only musts? Lashings of squirty cream and two spoons. Enjoy.

SERVES 2

3 scoops Vanilla Ice Cream (page 14)

3 scoops Dark Chocolate Ice Cream (page 21)

A chunk of Golden Honeycomb (page 160)

Chocolate sprinkles

4 tablespoons Glossy Hot Chocolate Sauce (page 154), at room temperature

Squirty (whipped) cream

Layer the ice creams in two sundae glasses with a medley of honeycomb and chocolate sprinkles. Pour over the chocolate sauce, squirt over a little cream and serve.

RHUBARB
CRUMBLE SUNDAE

Rhubarb and crumble is surely a match made in food heaven.
It's something to do with the slightly sour taste of the rhubarb coupled
with the sweetness of the crumble mix. Here, we've taken that winning
formula and popped it in a glass. Make this sundae with the first rhubarb
of the season for its pretty-as-a-picture pink colour.

SERVES 4

CRUMBLE

40g (1½oz) butter, at room
   temperature

50g (1¾oz) plain flour

40g (1½oz) rolled oats

30g (1oz) light soft brown sugar

RHUBARB COMPÔTE

400g (14oz) rhubarb, trimmed
   and cut into bite-sized chunks

2 tablespoons golden caster sugar

1 vanilla pod, slit in half
   lengthways

TO SERVE

12 scoops Rhubarb Ice
   Cream (page 32)

200ml (7fl oz) good-quality,
   ready-made cold custard

Preheat the oven to 180°C/fan 160°C/gas mark 4 and line a baking
sheet with baking parchment.

To make the crumble, put the butter and flour in a large mixing
bowl and rub together with your hands until the mix resembles
fine breadcrumbs. Stir through the oats and brown sugar. Pile the
mixture onto the prepared baking sheet and spread out evenly.
Transfer to the oven and bake for 20–25 minutes, until golden.
Remove from the oven and set aside to cool.

Meanwhile, make the compôte. Put the rhubarb in a medium
saucepan over a low heat with the sugar and vanilla pod. Cover
and cook gently for 8–10 minutes or until the rhubarb is tender
and has largely broken down. Remove from the heat, fish out
the vanilla pod and, using a teaspoon, scrape the seeds into the
compôte. Leave to cool to room temperature and, if needed, add
1–2 tablespoons of cold water to get a spoonable consistency.

To assemble the sundaes, add a spoonful of rhubarb compôte
to the base of four sundae glasses. Build up alternate layers of
crumble, ice cream, custard and compôte, finishing each glass
with a scoop or two of ice cream. Serve immediately.

KNICKERBOCKER GLORY

An unashamedly retro sundae, this recipe harks back to the days when kids' eyes popped out of their heads at the sight of tall sundae glasses filled to the brim with all manner of sweet treats. This glorious glory unites strawberries, marshmallows, vanilla ice cream and anything extra anyone fancies. There's a reason this recipe has stood the test of time – it elicits pure joy.

SERVES 2

6 strawberries, 4 hulled and halved and 2 left whole

2 tablespoons Strawberry Coulis (page 157)

6 scoops Vanilla Ice Cream (page 14)

6 Rose Marshmallows (page 164)

2 fan wafers

Place a strawberry half at the base of each sundae glass and pour over a little coulis. Top with a scoop of ice cream, then a marshmallow and repeat until all the ingredients have been used, reserving a whole strawberry for the top. Finish each with a fan wafer and serve immediately.

CHAPTER 5

CONES, SAUCES & TOPPINGS

We started out as straight up ice cream people, but over the years we've added ripples, toppings and other extras into the mix. Why? Because they're delicious, and they add a touch of razzmatazz. In this final chapter, we wanted to give you a chance to add extra colour, texture, flavour and more, at home, so we've developed a selection of toppings and sides especially for this book. They're crunchy, melty, salty, sweet, dense, light, swirling, scattered, brittle, pillowy, and everything else in between. Look out for our Waffle Cones (page 148) and the extremely pretty homemade Rose Marshmallows (page 164). With these winners up your sleeve, you'll never be short of ways to jazz up your ice cream.

WAFFLE CONES

Simple, effective and extraordinarily yummy, these are a brilliant DIY alternative to shop-bought cones. Be sure to work quickly when you're sculpting your homemade cones – they have been known to harden before your eyes! For extra joyful drama, try dipping these in sauces and sprinkles galore.

MAKES 8

3 medium egg whites

115g (4oz) golden caster sugar

75ml (2½fl oz) whole milk

25g (1oz) unsalted butter, melted

A pinch of salt

½ teaspoon vanilla extract

100g (3½oz) plain flour

Butter, for frying

TO DECORATE

75g (2¾oz) dark chocolate (minimum 70% cocoa solids), roughly chopped

Sprinkles, to dip

Put the egg whites, sugar, milk, butter, salt and vanilla extract into a large mixing bowl and beat together with a wooden spoon. Sift over the flour and mix in well. Continue to mix until the batter is smooth and the consistency of double cream.

Heat a non-stick frying pan over a low heat and add a small knob of butter. Use kitchen paper to wipe the melted butter around the surface of the pan.

Spoon 1 generous dessertspoon of batter into the pan and, using the back of a spoon, swirl around the pan into a thin, even circle roughly 15cm (6in) diameter. Cook for 2–3 minutes – the edges will start to brown and set. Flip the disc over and continue to cook on the other side for 1–2 minutes.

Working quickly, lift the disc from the frying pan and use a tea towel to protect your hands from the heat. Roll the bottom of the disc and shape into a cone, place it on a clean surface, seam side down, until it holds its shape. The cone will harden as it cools. Repeat to make 8 cones.

Melt the chocolate in a heatproof bowl set over a saucepan of simmering water or in the microwave. Dip the top section of the cooled cones in the melted chocolate and cover in sprinkles. Set the cones on baking parchment until the chocolate hardens.

These cones are best eaten on the day they are made. Any left over will keep in an airtight container for a day or two.

HOMEMADE WAFFLES
WITH **TWO TOPPINGS**

A simple recipe, with big results. The waffle mixture can even be made the day before, if you want to get ahead. You'll have plenty of chocolate chai syrup – enough for two days of waffles! And the yogurt ice cream is one of the easiest in the book, not to mention completely delicious. Finally, the finished article is a feast for the eyes. This delicious array is great for brunch parties where your guests can mix and match as they like.

MAKES 4–5 X 18CM (7IN) WAFFLES

5 medium eggs, separated

A pinch of salt

1 teaspoon ground cardamom
  or cinnamon

50g (1¾oz) unsalted butter,
  melted and cooled slightly

250ml (9fl oz) semi-skimmed milk

225g (8oz) plain flour

A little olive oil, for brushing

Put the egg yolks, salt and cardamom in a medium bowl and beat well with a wooden spoon. Stir in the melted butter. Pour in the milk and mix until fully incorporated. Gradually add the egg mixture to the sifted flour in another bowl and mix until you have a thick, uniform batter.

In a separate clean bowl, whisk the egg whites until stiff peaks form and then use a large spoon to fold them gently into the batter. Leave the batter to rest in the refrigerator for at least an hour but preferably overnight.

Heat an 18cm (7in) round waffle maker according to the manufacturer's instructions. Brush with a little oil and spoon a quarter of the batter into the waffle maker. Cook for 4–5 minutes and then serve with the topping of your choice.

YOGURT ICE CREAM, APPLE AND PLUM COMPÔTE AND WALNUTS

SERVES 4

YOGURT ICE CREAM
MAKES 700ML (1¼ PINTS)

100ml (3½fl oz) whole milk

1 tablespoon cornflour

500ml (18fl oz) full-fat Greek yogurt

125g (4½oz) golden caster sugar

A pinch of salt

A little lemon juice, to taste

COMPÔTE

600g (1lb 5oz) cooking apples,
  peeled, cored and roughly chopped

300g (10½oz) plums, halved

25g (1oz) soft dark brown sugar

½ teaspoon almond extract

For the ice cream, combine 2 tablespoons of the milk with the cornflour to make a paste. Slowly add the remaining milk and transfer to a small saucepan. Cook over a medium heat, stirring, for 3–4 minutes until almost simmering and steam rises from the surface. Remove the pan from the heat and set aside to cool.

Put the yogurt and sugar in a bowl. Stir for 2–3 minutes until the sugar has dissolved, then pour in the cooled milk, along with the salt and lemon juice. Stir to combine. Pour into an ice-cream machine and churn to a soft set following the manufacturer's instructions, or until the blade stops. Spoon the soft ice cream into an airtight, freezerproof container and freeze for at least 4 hours, or preferably overnight, until firm. Remove and allow the ice cream to soften for 5–10 minutes before scooping.

Meanwhile, for the compôte, put all the ingredients in a saucepan, cover and cook over a medium-low heat for 15 minutes, stirring occasionally. Remove from the heat once the fruit has broken down. Serve the waffles topped with compôte and ice cream.

CHOCOLATE CHAI SYRUP WITH STRAWBERRIES

SERVES 4
MAKES 225ML (8FL OZ)

125ml (4fl oz) whole milk

4cm (1½in) piece of fresh ginger,
  peeled and grated

2 cinnamon sticks

4–5 black peppercorns

6 cloves

5 green cardamom pods, bashed

2 whole star anise

50ml (2fl oz) double cream

100g (3½oz) dark chocolate,
  roughly chopped

300g (10½oz) strawberries hulled
  and halved, to serve

Put the milk, ginger, cinnamon, peppercorns, cloves, cardamom and star anise in a small pan and heat very gently for 10 minutes or so. Remove from the heat and allow the milk to cool to room temperature; the spices will continue to infuse the milk.

Strain the spices from the milk and return the milk to the pan along with the cream and chocolate. Again, heat over a gentle heat, stirring all the while, until the chocolate has melted and the sauce has become thick and glossy. Remove from the heat and pour onto the waffles laden with halved strawberries.

GLOSSY HOT CHOCOLATE SAUCE

We always say it, but good-quality chocolate is a must. Look for a bar with a high cocoa solids content and it will shine through in the finished article. Beating through cold butter at the end is a tried-and-tested technique for adding decadent, glassy glossiness. When you are ready to serve, simply dollop generously onto your scoop, dessert or sundae.

MAKES 250ML (9FL OZ)

200g (7oz) dark chocolate (minimum 70% cocoa solids), broken into pieces

200ml (7fl oz) whole milk

2 tablespoons double cream

30g (1oz) golden caster sugar

30g (1oz) cold butter, cubed

Put the chocolate into a heatproof bowl set over a saucepan of simmering water. Allow the chocolate to gently melt, stirring all the while.

Meanwhile, put the milk, cream and sugar in another saucepan and stir over a low heat until the sugar has dissolved. Once the chocolate has melted, pour into the warm milk mix and beat together. Remove from the heat and, using a wooden spoon, beat in the cold butter until the sauce is smooth and glossy. Serve straight away or leave to cool to room temperature before serving.

SALTED CARAMEL SAUCE

This sauce is heaven sent. No contest: it's the most luxurious topping for an ice cream. Make yours in advance and keep it in a jar in the refrigerator. Then gently reheat it in a small saucepan to turn it into molten gold and unleash those legendary flavours and textures. If you're not a fan of salt 'n' sweet, simply omit the salt from the recipe, but if you've never tried it, give it a go – it allows the caramel notes to sing.

MAKES 350ML (12FL OZ)

250g (9oz) golden caster sugar

180ml (6¼fl oz) cold water

40g (1½oz) butter

150ml (¼ pint) double cream

2–3 drops of vanilla extract

A pinch of sea salt flakes

Put the sugar and water in a medium heavy-based saucepan over a medium heat and allow the sugar to dissolve. Once the sugar has dissolved, increase the heat and gently boil. Do not stir the caramel at any stage, but swirl the pan lightly (this will help prevent the caramel from crystallizing on the sides of the pan). Once the caramel is a deep golden brown, remove from the heat and swirl in the butter. Working quickly, beat in the cream with a wooden spoon. Stir through the vanilla and sea salt flakes. Serve warm or at room temperature but not cold; the sauce becomes thick if left in the refrigerator.

 TIP: When making caramel, it's best not to select a non-stick pan because the surface tends to be dark or black, making it almost impossible to see the colour of the caramel develop, and the temptation will be to add the butter too early.

STRAWBERRY COULIS

A classic, vibrant coulis recipe, this is a happy-ever-after ending for overripe summer strawberries. The vanilla extract and lemon juice are optional; we love both additions, but your palate is in charge here, so do whatever you fancy. On a scoop, drizzled over a brownie, atop a cheesecake or in a sundae, this coulis is a winner, whatever's on your menu.

MAKES 350ML (12FL OZ)

50ml (2fl oz) cold water

25g (1oz) golden caster sugar

400g (14oz) strawberries, hulled and halved

½ teaspoon vanilla extract (optional)

A squeeze of lemon juice (optional)

Pour the water into a medium saucepan and stir in the sugar. Bring to a simmer over a medium heat and then drop the strawberries into the saucepan. Cook for 5–6 minutes until the strawberries collapse and soften. Remove from the heat and allow the sauce to cool for a couple of minutes. If using, stir through the vanilla extract and lemon juice. Using a stick blender, purée the mixture until smooth. Either pass it through a sieve to ensure a beautifully smooth coulis or leave it just as it is if you prefer. Cool, cover and store for up to 2 days in the refrigerator.

ROASTED SUMMER FRUITS

This topping adds beautiful colour and flavour to Vanilla Ice Cream (page 14) or Yogurt Ice Cream (page 151). It's vibrant, it's simple, and it's just perfect for the height of summer when soft fruits are at their best and most abundant.

SERVES 6

3 tablespoons clear honey

40g (1½oz) butter

1 vanilla pod, slit in half lengthways, or 2 teaspoons vanilla bean paste

A good pinch of sea salt

2 tablespoons amaretto

2 peaches, quartered and stoned

2 nectarines, quartered and stoned

200g (7oz) strawberries, hulled

40g (1½oz) almonds, roughly chopped

TO SERVE

Ice cream of choice

Preheat the oven to 200°C/fan 180°C/gas mark 6.

Put the honey, butter, vanilla, salt and amaretto in a small saucepan over a medium heat and cook until just bubbling.

Set the peaches and nectarines, cut side up, in a roasting tray and scatter the strawberries between them. Pour over the syrup and roast for 20 minutes until the fruit is soft.

Tip the almonds into a dry frying pan and fry over a medium-high heat until just toasted, about 2–3 minutes. Turn the nuts regularly and don't leave the pan unattended as nuts have a habit of burning. Once toasted, set the almonds aside.

Remove the roasted fruit from the oven and sprinkle with the toasted almonds. Serve warm, with a spoonful of syrup and a scoop of ice cream.

VEGAN DARK CHOCOLATE SAUCE

This sauce couldn't be simpler to make, or more delightful to indulge in. Keep any leftovers stored in the refrigerator and, when cravings announce themselves, warm a few spoonfuls in the microwave. It's the star of the show in our Vegan Peanut Butter Ice Cream (page 50). It's also an easy way to add extra indulgence to our Vegan Banana and Nut Butter scoop (page 47).

MAKES 300ML (½ PINT)

175ml (6fl oz) cold water

100g (3½oz) caster sugar

100g (3½oz) cocoa powder

¼ teaspoon salt

½ teaspoon vanilla bean paste

Put all the ingredients in a small saucepan and set over a medium heat. Cook for 6–8 minutes, stirring continuously with a wooden spoon, until velvety and smooth. Remove from the heat and continue to beat for 5 minutes until the sauce cools and becomes pourable and glossy. Transfer to a jug and either use immediately or cool before serving.

Store this sauce in the refrigerator for up to a week.

 TIP: If the sauce becomes stiff on cooling, simply reheat in the microwave in brief bursts so that it melts slightly, or spoon the sauce into a heatproof bowl and place over a pan of simmering water, stirring until soft and glossy.

GOLDEN HONEYCOMB

The bee's knees. This classic honeycomb is extremely handy. There are so many ways to use it: crumble it over a chocolate cake, stir it into our Dark Chocolate Ice Cream (page 21), scatter it over soft fruit or simply enjoy it as it is. It's a simple recipe made from store cupboard ingredients. And better still, it's like a kitchen science experiment. Kids will love watching the drama unfold. Keep the golden comb wrapped in an airtight box because when it's exposed to the air it goes tacky and soft.

FILLS A 20CM (8IN) SQUARE TIN

200g (7oz) golden caster sugar

100g (3½oz) golden syrup

2 teaspoons bicarbonate of soda

Start by lining a 20cm (8in) square tin with baking parchment. It is easiest to scrunch up a square of parchment into a ball, large enough to cover the base and sides of the tin. Unscramble the parchment, flatten slightly and simply drop into the tin, using your fingers to push it into the corners.

Put all of the caster sugar in a medium, clean saucepan. Pour over the syrup and heat over a medium-low heat. Gently stir to combine the ingredients until all molten and even. Once melted, increase the heat a little and bring the mixture to a bubble.

Simmer until the mixture is an amber colour, about 2 minutes. Remove from the heat and, working quickly, stir through the bicarbonate of soda with a wooden spoon. Swiftly beat until the bicarbonate has just disappeared, about 30 seconds, and then immediately pour the bubbling liquid into the lined tin. Be cautious as the mixture is boiling hot.

Leave the honeycomb to cool completely for 2 hours, before breaking it into chunks. Store in an airtight container between layers of baking parchment for up to a week.

GRANNY DORSEY'S GIGANTIC MERINGUES

We've mentioned Granny Dorsey's infamous meringues a few times in this book already, and with good reason. They are spectacular. This is a modern take on her classic recipe. Give it a thorough read before you get started – the steps here are slightly different from the usual method. The egg whites and sugar are warmed together in a bowl set over a pan of simmering water. This way, the sugar melts into the egg and 'cooks'. The result? A more stable, perfectly pliable mix that's ideal for sculpting giant meringues. These are a true staple in our family, and a highlight of our childhood. Three cheers for Jude's mum – Granny, you really knew how to make a Grade A meringue!

MAKES 6 LARGE MERINGUES

300g (10½oz) caster sugar

5 large egg whites, at
 room temperature

TOP TIP

This recipe is worth perfecting. It's the same method used for the meringues in our Frozen Eton Mess (page 93) and the Cinnamon and Winter Fruit Pavlova (page 99). Once you've got it down to a fine art, you're away!

Preheat the oven to 150°C/fan 130°C/gas mark 2. Line two baking sheets with baking parchment.

Put the sugar and egg whites in a large metal bowl and set over a pan of simmering water, ensuring that the base of the bowl is not in contact with the water. Cook for 5–7 minutes, scraping down the sides of the bowl and stirring occasionally with a rubber spatula, until the sugar has melted and the liquid is warm, smooth and slightly cloudy.

Pour this liquid into the bowl of a stand mixer or alternatively, use an electric handheld whisk. Whisk on high for 10–12 minutes until the meringue is cool to the touch and stands in stiff peaks.

Spoon onto the lined baking sheets in six large mounds. Transfer the sheets to the oven and immediately reduce the temperature to 120°C/fan 100°C/gas mark ½. Cook the meringues for 2 hours, until the outside is crispy and the inside is marshmallow-like. Cool completely on the baking sheets, then carefully peel off the paper.

The meringues can be eaten straight away or stored for up to a week in an airtight container.

TIP: This mixture can, of course, make meringues of many sizes. If you're after mini meringues, as for the Black and Blue Freakshake (page 126) or the Elderflower Celebration Cake (page 122), pile the mixture into a piping bag fitted with a small, plain nozzle and pipe onto a lined baking sheet. Reduce the cooking time to 1¼ hours and cool.

ROSE MARSHMALLOWS

There are few things as soft and precious-tasting as homemade marshmallows.
We love the hint of rose here, but if it isn't your cup of tea, simply omit.
Technically, these last 4–5 days when you store them in an airtight
container. In reality, they'll all be gobbled up before the day is done.

MAKES ABOUT 50

7 leaves of fine gelatine

200g (7oz) white granulated sugar

100g (3½oz) liquid glucose

2 teaspoons rosewater

Oil (sunflower), for brushing

DUSTING

75g (2¾oz) cornflour

75g (2¾oz) icing sugar

½ tablespoon pink food colouring

First, soak the gelatine. Measure 180ml (6¼ fl oz) cold water into a shallow bowl and add the leaves, one by one, to the water, fully immersing each one. Leave to soak for 10 minutes.

Heat the soaked gelatine and water in a small saucepan over a low heat for 3–4 minutes, until dissolved. Set aside until needed.

Put the granulated sugar, 5 tablespoons of the glucose syrup, the rosewater and 3 tablespoons of cold water into a medium, heavy-based saucepan and bring to the boil, stirring occasionally with a metal spoon. Continue for about 4–5 minutes, until a sugar thermometer shows 112°C (233°F), then pour the mixture into a large mixing bowl. Working quickly, add the remaining glucose syrup and mix on a low speed using an electric handheld whisk.

Whisking all the time, add the dissolved gelatine and its soaking liquid, then increase the speed to medium. Once the consistency of the mixture thickens, increase the mixer speed to maximum for a further 10–12 minutes until the mixture is thick enough to hold its shape on a whisk – it should have quadrupled in size and become marshmallow-like in appearance. The bowl will be almost cool to the touch.

Line a small roasting tin (roughly 30 x 20cm/12 x 8in) with clingfilm and brush thoroughly with oil. Spoon the marshmallow mixture into the tin and level with the back of an oiled spoon. Leave the marshmallow to set at room temperature for 4–6 hours or overnight.

Put the icing sugar and cornflour into a blender with the colouring and whizz until the colour has turned to a light pink, about 2 minutes, then tip into a bowl. Turn the marshmallow out of the tin using the clingfilm and cut into small cubes with a hot knife. Drop into the bowl, a piece at a time, and coat in the cornflour mix. The marshmallows will keep fresh for 4–5 days in an airtight container.

CHERRY, COCONUT AND BUCKWHEAT GRANOLA

This is a delicious staple to have on hand for breakfast and brunch alike. It makes for a beautiful and thoughtful homemade gift, too. Simply pop it in a jar, tie with a ribbon and add a label with a personal note. Serve your granola sprinkled over dark chocolate ice cream. Or dip an ice-cream cone right in and roll, for a generously crunchy topping.

MAKES 600G (1LB 5OZ)

250g (9oz) buckwheat kernals

200g (7oz) rolled oats

3 tablespoons sesame seeds

4 tablespoons coconut oil

4 tablespoons clear honey

½ teaspoon fine sea salt

1 teaspoon ground cinnamon

A little freshly grated nutmeg

50g (1¾oz) raisins

50g (1¾oz) dried cherries

30g (1oz) pumpkin seeds

25g (1oz) desiccated coconut

Preheat the oven to 180°C/160°C fan/gas mark 4 and line a large baking sheet with baking parchment.

Tip the buckwheat, oats and sesame seeds into a large mixing bowl. Put the coconut oil and honey in a small saucepan over a medium heat and warm for a minute or two until melted. Pour the warm liquid into the oat mixture and mix with the sea salt, cinnamon and nutmeg.

Spread the mixture on the lined baking sheet in an even layer, place in the centre of the oven and bake for 15 minutes. After that time break any lumps of granola up, shake it around and pop back in the oven for a further 10 minutes or until it is evenly golden brown and crunchy. Leave the mixture to cool completely on the baking sheet then break into bite-sized pieces and combine with the dried cherries, raisins, pumpkin seeds and coconut. Store in an airtight container for up to 2 weeks.

SALTED ALMOND PRALINE BRITTLE

Whether you opt for almond, pecan or peanut, a brittle improves many a pudding. Embrace the delicious mess and break yours up at the table. Guests can then dive in and choose a chunk or two. If you've been overzealous in cooking your caramel and it has a slightly burnt appearance, all is not lost. Once your darkened brittle has cooled and hardened, whizz it in a food processor to make caramel dust. It's perfect for sprinkling over ice cream, into crumbles and through yogurts.

SERVES 10–12
MAKES A 30 X 15CM (12 X 6IN) SLAB

50g (1¾oz) unsalted butter

185g (6½oz) granulated sugar

1 tablespoon cold water

180g (6¼oz) golden syrup

150g (5½oz) flaked almonds

1 teaspoon salt

Line a baking sheet with baking parchment and set aside. Set a small bowl of ice-cold water on the work surface, ready to test if the caramel is at the correct stage.

Put the butter, sugar, water and golden syrup in a medium heavy-based saucepan over a medium-high heat and bring to the boil. Add a sugar thermometer to the pan. Cook, gently swirling the pan, until the sugar begins to melt and turn golden, and the temperature reaches 150°C (300°F), hard crack stage. This should take about 6–8 minutes.

Remove from the heat and stir in the almonds. Pour the mixture onto the prepared baking sheet. Scatter with the sea salt and allow the brittle to cool, preferably overnight. Break into pieces to serve.

GINGERBREAD COWBARN

This is the template for the Gingerbread Cowbarn recipe on page 105. Templates are 50 per cent actual size.

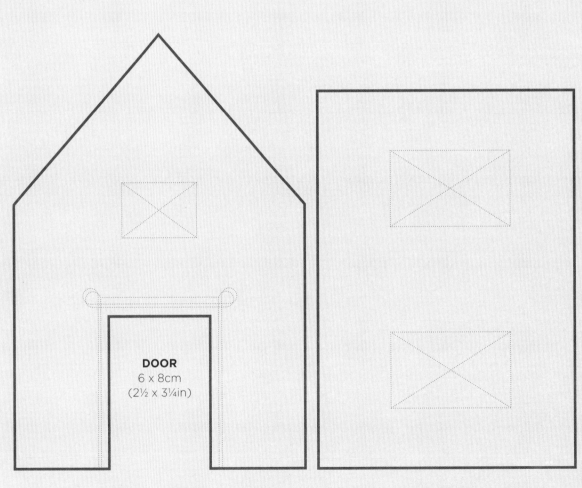

DOOR
6 x 8cm
(2½ x 3¼in)

2 X GABLE ENDS
14 x 16cm (5½ x 6¼in) including a triangle point
10 x 10.5 x 16cm (4 x 4⅛ x 6¼in)

2 X WALLS
14 x 20cm (5½ x 8in)

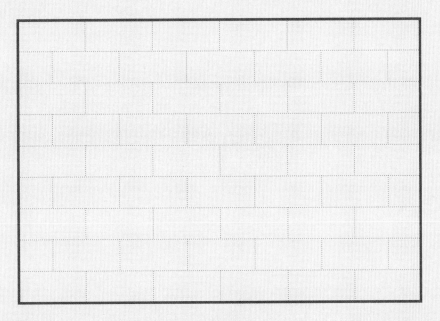

1 X ROOF
15 x 22cm (6 x 8½in)

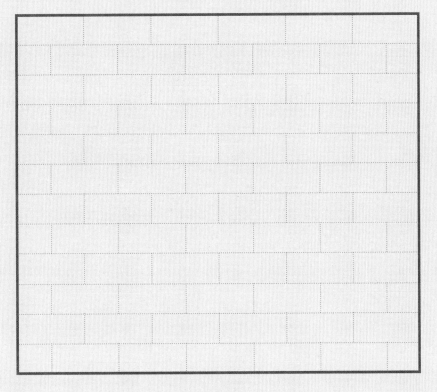

1 X ROOF
19 x 22cm (7½ x 8½in)